20th CENTURY EUROPE

20th CENTURY EUROPE

A Concise History

Arthur Drea

Arthur Drea

To order additional copies of this book, contact:
Xlibris Corporation
1-888-795-4274
www.Xlibris.com
Orders@Xlibris.com
117281

CONTENTS

DEDICATION

To my wife, Marilyn and my daughters,

Erin Olexia and Tracy McGowan

with love.

Acknowledgements

My first expression of gratitude goes to my friend and colleague, Bruce Knauff, for his tireless attention to editing the text, both technically and substantively. His corrections, additions, and suggestions have added immeasurably to the final result. Although best efforts were taken to avoid error, to the extent to which there are errors, they are wholly mine.

Heartfelt thanks also go to two other colleagues, the Doctors Schick and Hetfield, for their very generous comments on the back cover. Edgar Schick's remarks set the stage perfectly for the body of the work that follows.

Thanks, too, to the staff of the Maryland Public Library system, who were always eager and very capable of assisting in finding sometimes obscure reference materials.

My deepest appreciation, of course, goes to my wife, Marilyn, who in addition to being my own personal graphic designer, was on a daily basis my best encourager and valuable sounding board.

CHAPTER 1

Toward Disintegration (1895-1914)

European Imperialism

" I MPERIALISM" IS DEFINED by *The Dictionary of Human Geography* as, "The creation and maintenance of unequal economic, cultural, and territorial relationships." The major European nations, during the latter part of the 19th century, desired to control lands that had raw materials needed for expansion and development of industrial economies. There was also a constant need to open up markets abroad for the goods that were produced at home. Nationalism fed the drive for empires—nations often felt that gaining colonies was a measure of their greatness. Christian missionaries added to the other reasons for overseas expansion because of a strongly held view that European rule would end the slave trade and convert many native peoples to Christianity.

As a result of these factors, many European countries began to seize lands in Africa. Technology helped them to succeed. Steam engines, railroads, and telegraphs made it possible to penetrate deep into Africa and still have contact with the home country. Sophisticated weaponry, especially machine guns, gave the occupying forces far greater power than any African people possessed.

The British Empire was the largest and most populous empire in the history of the world. It included colonies of various sizes and complexities on all the inhabited continents, and gave rise to the expression, "the sun never sets on the British Empire." The British colonies were very profitable primarily because of the importation of great quantities of natural resources not found in Great Britain and the fact that the native people supplied a huge quantity of very inexpensive labor. Even after World War I, Britain remained connected to most self-governing countries, such as Canada, Australia, New Zealand, and South Africa. However, the so-called "jewel of the crown" was India with a population of some 300 million and colonial profits that far exceeded any other British colony. In addition, during time of war the colonies supplied many troops, exceeding those from Britain itself, to the war effort of the Empire.

In India the British created restrictions aimed at preventing India's economy from operating on its own. Imposed policies and laws required India to produce raw materials for British manufacturing and then to buy back the finished goods from Britain exclusively. These industries included textile production, salt processing, and agricultural produce such as rice. Indeed the massive exportation of many agricultural products caused substantial famines in the late 1800s.

However, by the opening of the 20th century, Britain's policies toward India improved somewhat. Government officials were instructed to have a hands-off policy toward Indian religious and social customs in spite of the fact that religious missionaries were aggressively seeking to convert the native population to Christianity. Furthermore, improvements in local technology were evident; the world's third largest railroad network was in operation along with many dams, bridges and irrigation canals. Sanitation and public health improved and schools and colleges were founded. British troops cleared central India of bandits and put an end to warfare among competing local rulers.

France was also an early colonizer in the 19th century, concentrating on North Africa (present-day Algeria, Tunisia and Morocco), as well as central Africa (present-day Nigeria) and the island of Madagascar. The French were among the first to create colonies in southeast Asia (present-day Viet Nam, Laos and Cambodia). The attitude of the French colonizers was more toward commercial exploitation and trade and less about political domination. Local leaders were used and accommodated more than the British did.

The Germans and Italians in the last part of the 19th century entered into the competition for colonies, mostly in north and eastern Africa. Germany had colonies in Africa that included portions of present-day Tanzania, Rwanda, Kenya, and Togo. Their principal Pacific island possessions were German New Guinea and German Samoa. German acquisition and expansion of colonies followed a plan and process with a minimum of friction with local leaders. Mercantile domination was always the key as opposed to large scale population expansion. Agreements were reached with other European nations, especially Great Britain, to share certain lands. However, only Togoland and German Samoa were profitable and self sufficient. In spite of this, German leadership persisted in supplying and defending its possessions.

Italian activities in the imperialist domain can be broken into two main parts. The first occurred during the "scramble for Africa" in the late 19th century and the early years of the 20th century. Italy, however, was at a substantial disadvantage to its European competitors because of a lack of financial strength. Only Eritrea and Somalia were acquired by the Italians during this period. Much later, in the 1930's, Mussolini was able to conquer and briefly hold Ethiopia, justifying in his mind a declaration on May 9, 1936 of an "Italian Empire."

Although there were tensions and disputes among the major European powers over African territory, the African war that caused the heaviest casualties and in many ways, marked the climax of imperialism on the continent, was not fought by whites against blacks but among the whites themselves. This was the Boer War in South Africa. This part of Africa was comprised of several "republics" with substantial independence but connected loosely to a central government of South Africa. In the 1890s the Boers (indigenous population) began to be threatened by the influx of immigrants, mostly British, who were attracted by the discovery of diamonds and gold. Cecil Rhodes (who later established the Rhodes Scholarship), was the Prime Minister of the Republic of Cape and a heavy investor in African mining.

He attempted in 1895 to unite the Republics in sympathy with the British against the Boers. Rhodes was overthrown, but the British pursued their interests and a full blown war began in 1899. It was a brutal war with many casualties on both sides, but it eventually ended in 1902. The legacy of mistrust and bitterness between Boers and Britons lasted for generations afterward. By 1914 virtually all of Africa had been claimed by one European power or another. The possession of colonies became part of the definition of a great power and the competition for colonies helped bring on World War I.

However, that tragic war weakened the major European countries, and the growing nationalistic desires of the colonial peoples made it very difficult, and eventually impossible, to maintain control. Demands for independence resounded around Africa and Asia, but it was not until after World War II that these demands were realized.

Military Arms Race and Alliances

Germany became committed to a powerful military under the leadership of Bismarck, the most influential German Prime Minister of the 19th century, who had engineered the unification of the Prussian States. Because of concern about Russia, Bismarck organized a Triple Alliance between Germany, Italy and Austria-Hungary in 1882. However, he was relieved as Chancellor in 1890 by the young Kaiser Wilhelm II, who was very ambitious and impatient to drive Germany to military superiority over arch rivals Russia, France, and especially Britain. The Kaiser already had the most powerful land army in Europe and wanted a navy to compare to the British navy, so he embarked on an unprecedented shipbuilding campaign after the turn of the century. Under Admiral Alfred Tirpitz the Imperial Naval Office began a long term shipbuilding program with the goal of overtaking the British navy in terms of capital warships. In 1900 Germany passed a Navy Law which increased the number of battleships from nine to twelve.

Britain had understood for centuries that its greatest security from foreign invasion lay with its sea power. The guiding principle was that to maintain naval superiority it would have to have a navy two and a half times larger than the next largest navy. In 1905 the British began construction of *Dreadnaught* (literally "fear nothing"), the largest and most powerful battleship ever produced at that time. Dreadnaught battleships were large, fast, heavily armored, and contained ten 12-inch guns. They were virtually impregnable, but of course other countries could also, over time, produce them. Thus, came about the very definition of a naval arms race.

The leading figure in Britain guiding this naval development was the First Sea Lord, Admiral John Fisher. It was under his direct management that *Dreadnaught* was built and many smaller cruisers were constructed. For political and economic reasons, however, Britain was anxious to substantially reduce naval armament building and end the race that the launching of *Dreadnaught* created. A proposal to that effect was sent to Germany in 1911 and responded to personally by Tirpitz: "Here is England, already more than four times as strong as Germany, in alliance with Japan, and probably so with France, and you, the colossus, come and ask Germany, the pigmy, to disarm. From the point of view of the public it is laughable . . . and we shall never agree to anything of the sort." After this unambiguous rebuff, Britain and France negotiated a secret naval alliance intended to buttress French naval security in the Baltic and Mediterranean Seas.

　ARTHUR DREA

Germany kept pace and by 1911 had eleven Dreadnaught class battleships and Britain had eighteen. Similar arms development was going on with France and Italy with their land armies and weaponry. Germany widened and dredged the Kiel Canal from the Baltic to the North Sea to allow passage by its new, large battleships. Britain also built new naval bases for its capital ships, particularly at Scapa Flow in northern Scotland. This location was highly strategic because the German ships would need to go well north around Scotland to reach the Atlantic.

The French were greatly alarmed by this military activity in Germany, including a universal conscription, so they negotiated with Russia and in 1894 achieved the Franco-Russian Entente (an agreement of less force than a treaty between friendly nations). Britain later, in 1907, joined the Entente with France and Russia, creating the Triple Entente to counter the Triple Alliance of Germany, Italy and Austria-Hungary established years before by Bismarck.

Military war planning goes on constantly whether war seems imminent or not. So Germany had such a war plan for western Europe called the Schlieffen Plan. General Alfred von Schlieffen was the undisputed military planner for Germany during the last years of the 19th and first years of the 20th centuries. He described his plan simply as, "The heart of France lies between Brussels and Paris." He developed a plan by 1906 calling for a massive ground force to move west through Belgium and then southwest to Paris. Other movements were essentially diversions in the south against French territory. The Schlieffen Plan remained unchallenged right up to the opening of hostilities in 1914.

Both the French and British were aware of the general aspects of the Schlieffen Plan but did not believe it would be politically possible to implement because Belgium was firmly neutral and its neutrality was guaranteed by both France and Britain. Invading Belgium would immediately widen the war. The French also believed that their long and well fortified line of defenses on their eastern border would stop or greatly impede any German advance. Both assumptions proved false very quickly after hostilities began in August of 1914.

East of Germany, Russia was viewed as vast and containing millions of potential soldiers but woefully unprepared. Worse still, the country had completely inept leadership on both the civil and military sides. Historian Barbara Tuchman describes Czar Nicholas II in strong terms: "The regime was ruled from the top by a sovereign who had but one idea of government—to preserve intact the absolute monarchy bequeathed to him by his father-and who, lacking the intellect, energy or training for his job, fell back on personal favorites, whim, simple mulishness and other devices of the empty-headed autocrat." French reliance on the Russians' delaying many German divisions in the east was not a widely shared opinion, and, as it turned out, France had misjudged badly.

So the alliances meant by some to prevent war, along with the arms race, were making war almost inevitable. The Kaiser and his ministers were very aggressive and bellicose in their communications and responses to proposals from the British for moratoria on arms buildup (as noted in the Tirpitz comments above). The Germans believed that the British were patronizing and simply wanted to maintain naval superiority at little expense. However, Wilhelm actually had made Germany's tactical situation far worse by alarming powerful and unfriendly nations to the east-Russia, and the west—France and Britain. A spark was all that was needed, but the actual spark was one that could not have been predicted by anyone.

CHAPTER 2

World War I and Its Immediate Aftermath (1914-1919)

Minor Event Triggers Military Obligations

MANY AND VARIOUS groups, especially in Eastern Europe, such as anarchists, nationalists, and communist revolutionaries, were organizing against the established order. In Serbia, which bordered Austria-Hungary to the south, there were especially strong feelings against Austria-Hungary because of the latter's domineering approach to its smaller neighbors and because of significant language differences.

When Archduke Ferdinand of Austria-Hungary, the heir to the empire's throne, visited Sarajevo, the capital of Bosnia and officially a part of Austria-Hungary, on June 28, 1914, he and his wife were assassinated by a young revolutionary who had been trained and equipped in Serbia. The Austria-Hungarian government quickly blamed Serbia. Although the Archduke was not popular in Austria because he had favored a republican form of government that would have raised the status of Slavs in Austria, he was, nevertheless, killed by someone who would have undoubtedly supported this policy had he known it. There are great ironies in precipitous violent actions.

As previously indicated, the Triple Alliance, created in 1882, consisted of Germany, Italy and Austria-Hungary. The Germans believed they were morally, if not legally, required to assist Austria in any international disputes. The Austrians were uncertain of German support, but their concern was not Serbia. It was Russian sympathy for Serbia. The Russians responded angrily to Austria's unreasonable demands, which amounted to loss of independence, and their ultimate declaration of war on Serbia on July 28, 1914. There were strong Slavic relationships between Russia and Serbia as well as other ethnic and religious connections between them. The Russians partially mobilized their army near the Austrian-Russian border. On July 30th the Austrians ordered general mobilization of their military. (In the early 20th century mobilization of a country's military was often viewed as a declaration of war.)

The German General Staff had been concerned as far back as 1905 with the untapped military potential of the huge population of Russia. The leading Army General, Helmut von Moltke, urged an early, decisive war with Russia while it was still weak and unprepared. Not all in the German government were in favor of war with Russia, but Wilhelm, who was still the final authority on these matters, was very close to and supported his General Staff. He viewed national obligations as questions of honor for the country. In addition, German planning for military mobilization was very advanced and could be accomplished much faster than that of any other European nation. Germany also understood that France was not likely, in view of its obligations to Russia, to stand by and allow a quick defeat of Russia by Germany, thus establishing Germany and its ally Austria as the dominant force in continental Europe. Because of these reasons and his personal desire for grandeur, Wilhelm declared war on Russia on August 1, 1914.

The Schlieffen Plan, previously discussed, anticipated many of these situations involving the two front war. It prescribed the bulk of the German forces to first invade France, the more powerful of the two countries, while holding the Russians in the east to a stable or slowly advancing front. The Schlieffen Plan also envisioned invading France through Belgium, a neutral country. As mentioned, Belgian neutrality had been guaranteed by both France and Britain some years before. The question for the Germans was, would Britain enter a major war to defend Belgium or France? Germany's reliance on a military plan devised more than a decade earlier was one of the major miscalculations of the prewar period.

The Triple Entente at this time consisted of agreements of support between Russia, France and Britain. So by August 1st, Russia was faced with a major war with Germany and Austria. From the first days of the war, France was encouraging Russia to open a vigorous front in the east to relieve a major buildup of German divisions on the Belgian and French borders. The Russians promised a large offensive to begin by August 14; however, they had made no preparations for such an early date and predictable problems of communications, transportation, and continuing supply developed immediately. Indeed, in 1914 the Russians had only 418 motorized transport vehicles and 320 airplanes, but few qualified pilots. Despite, the Russians' initial successes with veteran troops in East Prussia and along the Austrian border, their supply problems became insurmountable and forced quick retreats.

By the end of July, the French military and much of the political leadership believed that war with Germany was imminent. German troops were assembled *en mass* at both the northern and southern borders between the two countries, and alarmingly, along the Belgian border. In addition to urging the Russians to take prompt and aggressive action, the French were pressuring the British to make it clear that they would enter the war against Germany if there was an invasion of France through Belgium.

The commanding French General was Joseph Jacques-Joffre, who was demanding that his government authorize mobilization and movement of troops to the borders. On July 30th he told the leaders that if his demands were not met immediately the Germans would, ". . . enter France without firing a shot." Finally, at 4:00 pm on August 2, 1914, the French government authorized full mobilization and France prepared for all out war with Germany.

Even then the British were not willing to face what had become a *fait accompli*. There was a split among the British Cabinet, stemming from the Boer War, between the imperialists such as Prime Minister Henry Asquith, Foreign Secretary Edward Grey, and First Lord of the Admiralty Winston Churchill, and the isolationists who feared foreign entanglements. Most political leaders on both sides would not have supported a war simply to defend France, but the moral outrage of the threatened invasion of tiny Belgium was a more unifying cause. The first preliminary vote of the Cabinet on August 1st on the issue of an ultimatum to Germany against any encroachment into Belgium was a sound defeat of the proposition. Those who lost this initial decision were confident that Germany would very soon invade Belgium and thereby change the political calculus in the Cabinet. They were proved to be correct.

A week or so before, the British fleet had been conducting previously scheduled exercises and were due to disperse very soon. Churchill requested permission to keep the fleet and its personnel together, but he was denied. In a bold move, which suggested his later propensity for independent action, Churchill, with the secret approval of Foreign Secretary Grey, kept the fleet together and sent them to their war stations in Scapa Flow, Scotland. They were thus well prepared to resist any early movement by the German navy out to the North Sea.

On August 2nd, the French requested through diplomatic channels that the British respond to their concern that the German navy might appear in the Channel and threaten French ports. The British did respond that they would give all protection in their power to prevent this, but even this action would not require the British to declare war. Two days later the German army crossed the Belgian border and formally began the war. Later that evening, an ultimatum was sent to Germany demanding removal of German forces from Belgium. Receiving no reply by midnight of the 4th, the British formally declared war on Germany.

Consequently, the creation of the Triple Alliance and the Triple Entente, meant by many to preserve the peace in Europe, actually resulted in a very sudden escalation involving five major powers. The greatest fear of Germany's Bismarck of a two front war was in fact realized. Germany faced Russia to the east and France and Britain to the west.

Allied vs. Axis Powers

The two sides now referred to as "Allied" (Britain, France and Russia) and "Axis" (Germany and Austria) were very well balanced militarily. The Axis powers, primarily Germany, had the strongest land forces and the best strategy. The Allied powers had greater financial strength, greater numbers, and the strongest naval forces, primarily British.

The Germans began their long planned offensive on August 4, 1914, by invading Belgium, and the "Great War" had begun. The Schlieffen Plan was followed precisely but the Belgians did not cooperate—they resisted fiercely and slowed the German advance. The Kaiser was reportedly shocked that the Belgians did not roll over and accept German domination. Still by early September the German northern force was within sight of Paris. The opposing forces were generally separated by the River Marne to the northeast of Paris. The French fought a desperate, defensive battle to protect their beloved capital city and stopped the German advance.

The Anglo-French military leaders and their German opponents concentrated heavily on the Western Front, certain that the next time around, "with one more push," they could achieve a breakthrough. As a result, the lives of millions of men were sacrificed. Even on ordinary days, when the Western Front was mostly quiet, many soldiers died on reconnaissance missions and by shellings. Both sides launched gigantic offenses, but at best these gained a few useless miles. Thereafter, the war in the west became the trench warfare for which World War I is most remembered.

During the next four years there were many large battles, but few of them had much impact on the ultimate outcome of the war, except for the massive loss of life on both sides. Although the Allies had greater losses than the Axis powers, the latter had fewer men to draw from. There are two battles that are worthy of mention because of their overall historical importance: the Battle of Gallipoli and the naval Battle of Jutland.

At the end of 1914 the war was not going well for the Allies, and the proud British navy had had virtually no activity. Churchill, the First Lord of the Admiralty, devised a plan to attack the Dardanelles, the narrow opening between the Mediterranean Sea and the Sea of Marmora which then opened to the Black Sea. The Turks had aligned themselves with the Germans and were providing harbor and safety to German warships in the Black Sea. If the British could capture the Dardanelles they could cut off this protection and supply the Russians in the north of the Black Sea. The land area protecting the Dardanelles is Gallipoli, a high position overlooking the narrows with Turkish gun positions facing the sea. Churchill convinced the Cabinet that Gallipoli could be taken with naval gunfire alone, without the need of ground troops. From February 19, 1915 to March 18th five battleships, four British and one French, bombarded Gallipoli with long range naval guns without discernable effect. Meanwhile the Turks had mined the narrows. After a long intensive bombardment on the 18th, the British tried to force the narrows. All the Allied ships hit mines and were either destroyed or severely damaged, requiring them to withdraw.

There were further efforts to use ground forces, mostly *ANZAC* troops from Australia and New Zealand, but the Turks under the command of Mustafa Kamal repelled all efforts to capture the peninsula. Kamal was later named "Ataturk," the father of modern Turkey. (See Chapter 3.)

Jutland

Jutland is an area in the north of Denmark which faces west to a large expanse of the North Sea. By 1916, the German Navy had largely been bottled up, except for submarines, by the British Navy. The only way for the Germans to get to the Atlantic to attack British shipping was to go north past Denmark and around Scotland. This was hazardous because the British were vigilant to spot any German ships. The British fleet, known as the Grand Fleet, was stationed at three ports in Scotland, with Scapa Flow in the north being the main port. The British were under the overall command of Admiral John Jellicoe. The German fleet was known as the

High Seas Fleet and was entirely stationed at Heligoland in the north of Germany. The Germans were commanded by Vice Admiral Reinhard Scheer. The two day Battle of Jutland, on May 31 and June 1, 1916 was the largest and last great naval battle consisting primarily of surface ships firing heavy guns from great distances. (Of course, other significant naval battles occurred in World War II but they were dominated by aircraft carriers and airplanes.)

The Grand Fleet came down from Scotland in six rows of four battleships in each row, accompanied by battle cruisers, destroyers and service ships. They were hunting for the High Seas Fleet which they had reliable information had left their home port in large numbers. The High Seas Fleet nearly matched the British in Dreadnaught size battleships with 22 to the British 24. Early in the afternoon of May 31st, scouting parties from each side spotted the other and there were minor skirmishes, but it was not until 5:30 pm that the main bodies encountered each other, first by the faster battle cruisers and destroyers. But within an hour, the British had two battleships seriously damaged, one sunk, and the Germans had two destroyed. By nightfall the High Seas Fleet was attempting to escape the British by maneuvering behind them and then racing to the east. There were further distant encounters with light damage in the early morning hours of the 1st, but by 3:30 am the High Seas Fleet had reached the safety of Horns Reef in Denmark.

There were recriminations on both sides and, in the end, the losses in capital ships and personnel were about equal, with the British losing somewhat more. The immediate result of the Battle of Jutland was the elimination of the German surface navy from the rest of the war. The long term historical lesson of the battle, which was not learned by most traditional naval planners for several decades, was the obsolescence of large surface gun platforms in air dominated warfare.

The Russian Collapse in the East

The Russian Government, in looking back to the days of Napoleon, believed that the key to their military success was the mobilization of a huge army which could then overwhelm any force attempting to invade. So in less than a year, the Russian army numbered nearly 10 million men, but they were woefully short of everything: officers, training facilities, weapons, food and virtually all necessities of an army in the field.

Throughout the war, it was common for an advancing army to supply only front line troops with rifles, with the following soldiers being required to pick up the weapons of those in front who had died. The condition of civilians was also desperate, with food and fuel shortages creating an ungovernable black market and complete disregard for any attempts by government to ration necessities. By 1917 human losses were staggering even by Russian standards. Over 650,000 had died and 2,500,000 were wounded in a hopeless war that few participants even understood. Constant labor unrest, added to virtual bankruptcy of the government and no reasonable leadership on the horizon, clearly offered opportunities to any revolutionary minded groups, of which there was no shortage. On March 15th, the Tsar was forced to abdicate and a Provisional Government was created which pledged to end the war on honorable terms. But it was far too late. Thousands of soldiers and whole units were streaming home to be greeted by famine and poverty. Discipline evaporated, and the war against Germany in the east simply ceased to exist.

Germany could not take full advantage of this collapse because it was also strained to the limit in fighting a two front war. However, important Russian industrial sites were seized and, in March 1918, Germany offered what amounted to a surrender document (the Treaty of Brest-Litovsk) to the Bolshevik Government and then removed all but one million men from the eastern front to the west. With this new influx of men in the west, the Germans made impressive advances and by July were again at the Marne River, approximately 35 miles from Paris.

Although the United States had declared war on Germany in April of 1917, significant numbers of U.S. troops were not available in Europe until June of 1918. They immediately provided a decisive fresh force. The American Expeditionary Force, as it was called, was commanded by General John Pershing who made no friends among the Allied commanders when he refused to allow American soldiers to be commanded by anyone other than American officers. His view was that the British and French commanders had made a mess of the war up to that point.

The German advance into France the second time was quick, but its retreat was also very rapid. Allied and American counteroffensives were well planned and German supplies and reserves were basically depleted. The German commander, General Erich Ludendorff, saw the inevitable collapse of the German fighting force, so he sought peace terms directed primarily at President Woodrow Wilson of the United States. This was a prudent move because Wilson and the U.S. had not suffered nearly as much as the other Allied countries and would probably have been less vindictive in setting peace terms. Moreover, Wilson was known as an idealist who generally opposed war and had set out in writing his general principles to guide any post war discussions. The Allies agreed to an Armistice which was not a surrender but a formal cease fire. It was agreed that the parties would return to the national boundaries that existed at the beginning of the war and that all fighting would cease at the eleventh hour of the eleventh day of the eleventh month in 1918.

Armistice and Paris Peace Conference

After the Armistice was declared on November 11, 1918, the guns were quiet but the worst military carnage in world history, even to this day, was far from over. The parties awaited a meeting planned for Paris in January of 1919. The chiefs of state of Great Britain, France, Italy and the United States gathered in Paris to begin discussing how to remake the world. Their views were very idealistic in believing that they had just experienced the "war to end all wars." They were guided by certain principles to which they nominally agreed, and these are generally summarized as the Fourteen Points, offered by President Wilson. British Prime Minister David Lloyd George and France's Premier Georges Clemenceau dominated the early conversations about a Peace Treaty, and much of that conversation centered around retribution against Germany for, in the opinion of the Allies, starting the war unnecessarily. The Germans, of course, did not believe they were responsible for the war and strongly resisted the accusation.

The three principals, Lloyd George, Clemenceau, and Wilson discussed new borders, reinstatement of former countries, abolition of some colonies, and consolidation of common language areas, among many other points. Although the original principal group included Vittorio Orlando of Italy, he was rather quickly sidelined by the other three because of Italy's relatively lesser role in the war and Orlando's complete fixation on Italy's demands to control Croatia and the northeastern portion of the Adriatic. The other three presented a significant contrast in personalities. Both the British and French people had been told that Germany would be forced to pay for the war in territorial losses as well as huge reparations to be paid to Allied countries. Consequently, this view represented the public positions of Clemenceau and Lloyd George.

Clemenceau was the oldest of the three and France had suffered the most of the three countries. Also, France had a longer history of aggression by Germany, so he was the most adamant about weakening Germany in every conceivable way. Lloyd George was in a difficult political position because while his public comments and the sentiments of British citizens conformed to those of France, he was extremely concerned about the Russian Revolution and believed that Germany was the only country that could serve as a barrier to the spread of communism. Wilson was also a strong anti-communist, but his overriding opinion was that "self determination," (a term he devised) by native peoples was the best safeguard against future wars. In addition, Wilson placed unrealistic hope in the proposed League of Nations to negotiate and settle all international disputes short of war.

To bring these three, and many other world leaders, together in the short time frame of six months that had been agreed upon, was virtually impossible. Of course, the Germans were excluded from all considerations of the Peace Treaty. As a practical matter, Germany had already relinquished all territory it had conquered since 1914 and specifically agreed to renounce all claims to Alsace-Lorraine. But the new government of Germany believed that many other issues such as colonies, national defense, and amounts of reparations were still open to discussion. They were to be shocked and gravely disappointed.

In June of 1919, a diplomatic note in unusually strong terms for diplomacy, expressed the outrage of the German Government: "Yielding to overpowering might, the government of the German Republic declares itself ready to accept and to sign the peace treaty imposed by the Allied and Associated governments. But in so doing, the government of the German Republic in no wise abandons its conviction that <u>these conditions of peace represent injustice without example.</u>" (emphasis added). Here was an omen of things to come?

A summary of the Versailles Treaty is beyond the scope and purpose of this work but Germany's principal losses are important to consider, especially because they were used only a few years later to buttress the fascist regime of Adolf Hitler. As noted above, Germany relinquished all claims to Alsace-Lorraine, an area on the border with France that had about an equal number of German and French speaking citizens. Furthermore the border area west of the Rhine in German territory was to maintain a 50 kilometer demilitarized zone.

Permanent disarmament of Germany eliminated all warships except small coastal boats, and the standing army could not exceed 100,000 men. All warplanes, tanks, heavy artillery, and poison gas were prohibited. Reparations for starting an unjust war, a particularly sensitive issue, were set, after much discussion, at $5 billion each of the next two years and a final figure to be agreed upon for the next 30 years. Most of the German colonies were either eliminated or required to be shared with other European countries.

The two territorial pretexts Germany most relied upon in the 1930s to justify the beginning of World War II were the loss of the Czech-Slovak land in the east and the reestablishment of an independent Poland bordering East Prussia. Poland was also given access to the Baltic through the newly internationalized free city of Danzig (present day Gdansk). All of these territories had been German at least since the days of Bismarck. The Germans believed, with some justification, that these lands had been well assimilated into the German Empire before the World War I, and were not causes of contention at the beginning of that war.

This one-sided Treaty satisfied very few in 1919, and it is literally true that the ink was not dry before efforts were underway, especially in the East and South, to change many of those decisions.

CHAPTER 3

Turkish Revolt and Irish Independence

Mustafa Kamal Ataturk—Turkish Independence

IT IS NOT often that history can ascribe to one individual the credit for changing the direction of national, and even international, governments affecting millions of people, but such is the case with Mustafa Kamal Ataturk. (His given name was Mustafa Kamal, but the appellation "Ataturk," meaning Father of Turkey was given to him later by the Turkish people.) The relatively young military officer of the Ottoman Turks gained initial fame by leading the Turkish defense at Gallipoli in 1915 against the British assault to control the Dardanelles. But it was just after the war that Kamal began his most important activities to encourage the collapse of the Ottoman Empire and to create an independent and secular Turkey.

The once proud and powerful Ottoman Empire had been declining for more than a century, but the end of World War I was truly the death throes of what was left of the Empire. The collapse of the German offensive in July of 1918 and the destruction of large areas of Eastern Europe, formerly under the control of the Empire, added to the millions of deserters, made clear to the Ottoman leaders that the end of the Empire was at hand. Prior to the Peace Conference, some small hope was held for Woodrow Wilson and his apparent benevolent approach to existing nationalities and historic connections. But that last hope was dashed when, in January of 1919, Wilson called for the Empire to be dismembered and divided into sectors effectively under the control of the victors.

The Greeks, unlike the Ottomans, had chosen the right side in the war and were therefore aggressively asserting their claims to the eastern side of the Aegean and Mediterranean Seas, particularly the City of Smyrna (present day Izmir). Although the Turkish population was in the majority, the region was controlled by the Greek army after the war. The Greeks made a strong case to the big three in Paris that Smyrna was necessary economically and militarily to protect the Greek islands and eastern border of Greece from possible attacks by the more populous Turks. The British, French and American leaders listened almost exclusively to the Greeks, and in May 1919 they authorized the Greeks to occupy Smyrna and the coastal regions in far greater military numbers. The western leaders also feared that left-wing movements, including Bolshevism, would take a strong hold in areas of eastern Europe and that the Greeks were probably the best resistance to those movements. Indeed, there were communist sympathizers and many socialists in the remnants of the Ottoman government and all were seeking a powerful leader. But it is also fair to say that most of the Arab world saw three Christian men deciding arbitrarily, and in their own interests, the makeup and future of the Muslim world.

Mustafa Kamal was emerging after the war as a principal leader against partition of the Empire. He was one of the first to recognize that Allied diplomacy was completely at odds with the overwhelming Turkish opinion supporting independence. Kamal sought authority in the Imperial Government, nominally headed by the Sultan, and was given a military and civilian leadership position in Anatolia. He immediately began resistance activities against both the Greek occupation and his Imperial Government authority. When he was ordered to return to Istanbul, he refused and was discharged. Henceforth, he became a fully committed leader of a growing resistance movement.

The Turkish nationalists, as the resistance movement became popularly known, grew in numbers, and, with the material and covert support of the French, became an effective military force under leaders who had gotten experience in the war. Kamal was their popular and undisputed commander. As the military situation deteriorated for the Allies, a decision led by the British was made to allow the Greek army to move inland with the ultimate goal of occupying Constantinople. The nationalists melted back into the interior but remained organized. By August 1920, the Greeks had moved 250 miles into the interior. A counterattack the following month by the nationalists halted the Greek advance but failed at that point to drive the Greeks back. However, Kamal had protected his eastern and southern borders and was free to concentrate on moving north and west against the Greeks. A stalemate developed and during that time the Greek government collapsed and was replaced by a monarchy. Kamal utilized this time by successfully reaching agreements with the Bolshevik government in Russia, with the Italians, and with the French. The terms of these agreements all differed but they each secured Kamal's nationalists from fear of attacks by more powerful potential adversaries. The Greeks, encouraged by Lloyd George's government, organized a large force in August of 1921 to assault Ankara which was the center of nationalist strength and Kamal's headquarters. After three bloody weeks of fighting, the Greeks were forced to retreat and were never again the superior force in Turkey.

The British had been occupying Constantinople and the Dardanelles with a nominal force since the end of the war but now could see a substantial army developing to the south and west. The nationalist army had the overwhelming support of the Turkish people and represented a huge struggle even for the British. Lloyd George urged war with the nationalists to retain those sites that the Peace Conference had given to Britain to defend. However, his Cabinet did not agree and, more importantly, the British people, exhausted by a terrible war, would not have supported a new war.

Kamal moved quickly while the British pondered what to do. On August 26, 1922, Turkish forces launched a powerful attack on the Greeks all along the Mediterranean coast. The Greeks suffered a devastating defeat and were forced to evacuate from Smyrna under heavy assault.

The Turks did not cover themselves with glory after the victory because much horrible vengeance was meted out to those Greeks remaining. Kamal pressed his advantage by moving north to the outskirts of Constantinople. He prudently halted and awaited the British decision.

Lloyd George's government was defeated in November 1922 because of this issue of potential war and other matters. The British commander in Constantinople refused to fire on the Turks, and that made the question to negotiate even easier to make. By late 1922 Mustafa Kamal was very famous throughout both the eastern and western worlds and was beloved by most Turks. He was on the brink of creating a fully independent Muslim nation in a world dominated by Christian powers. There was even a small movement to name him the new Sultan, but this concept completely contradicted his beliefs and purposes. Still, the six centuries old sultanate was revered by many so Kamal expressed his views in no uncertain terms: "The reason you do not find the Greek king among our prisoners of war is that royal sovereigns are inclined to partake only of their nation's pleasures. In times of catastrophe, they think of nothing but their palaces."

But the matter of the Sultan was complicated because the symbolic religious leader in Islam was the caliph, whose position had been fused with the sultanate several centuries earlier. To abolish the Sultanate it would be necessary to separate the caliphate, which had no governmental authority, from the Sultan. The Turkish Grand National Assembly, of which Kamal was the undisputed leader, debated this question of separation until Kamal again expressed a clear direction: "Now the Turkish nation . . . seizes its own sovereignty. This is a fait accompli. If the Assembly accepts this naturally, it would be better in my opinion. If not, this truth will be expressed in due course, although probably some heads will be cut off." Debate ended immediately and the proposal to separate the caliphate from the Sultanate passed quickly. These unambiguous and threatening remarks foretold the autocratic form of governance intended by Mustafa Kamal. The Sultan was allowed to be exiled on a British warship in November of 1922.

With the signing of the Lausanne Peace Treaty on July 24, 1923, most of the decisions made in Paris in 1919 dealing with the Ottoman Empire were undone, and the new independent Turkish Nation was recognized by all the world powers. Until his death in 1938, Kamal energetically moved his new nation to be more westernized in virtually every way. These reforms included: adoption of the Gregorian calendar; banning the Ottoman script; adoption of a constitution requiring a western style legal system; encouragement of western style dress for men and women; support for the emancipation of women, including the right to vote and hold office by 1930; and major changes in the quality of education, particularly in science and technology. In November of 1934, the Turkish Grand National Assembly honored Kamal with the surname "Ataturk," to be properly known from that point forward as "Mustafa Kamal Ataturk."

Turkey in more recent years has become a powerful nation and member of NATO (North Atlantic Treaty Organization). It remains the only truly secular government in the Islamic world and may soon become a full member of the European Union.

Irish Independence

The struggle for the independence of Ireland from Great Britain did not begin in the 20th century but had been going on, unsuccessfully, for several centuries. Our consideration here will cover this continuing effort from the Easter Rising of 1916 to the conclusion of the Irish Civil War in 1923.

There never was unanimity of opinion among the Irish about what "independence" really meant. Prior to World War I, there probably was a majority of Irish citizens who would have been satisfied, at least for several years, with Home Rule. This term was understood by most to mean obtaining a considerable level of local governmental autonomy, exercised by locally elected representatives, but with Ireland remaining fully included within the British Empire. The British Parliament would continue to have ultimate authority but would cede all local matters to an Irish Parliament. Efforts to achieve this change were nearly successful at the end of the 19th century, but with Britain becoming more absorbed with growing war concerns, lesser issues like Irish Home Rule (lesser from the British perspective) were put on the shelf for a later time.

Of course, there were also many Irish who believed that the meaning of independence was just that, complete separation from Britain and total autonomy of government in Ireland. Those who felt this way often referred back many years to American independence where important similarities could be drawn. The opponent, Britain, was the same; the objective was the same, total independence; and success was only achieved after a long and difficult war.

There was also a split of opinion about the necessary means to achieve either of these objectives. The Home Rule advocates tended to believe in a non-violent political process, achieving success in a slower step by step approach. The independence fighters, generally referred to as the IRB (Irish Republican Brotherhood), believed that the British would never voluntarily give up any significant control over Ireland. Both sides had considerable evidence in past history to support their views. But Irish history also taught that the time to press Britain for concessions or ultimate independence was when Britain was involved with other serious matters, like a world war.

So it was that the IRB, and other related organizations, chose 1916, the middle of World War I, to seize government buildings in Dublin, principally the General Post Office. A Proclamation of Independence was read from the building on April 24, 1916, and that date, like the American 4th of July, is considered the birth date of the Irish Republic. The Proclamation was written by Padraic Pearse, a young scholar and poet. The British had the resources to put down the uprising in less than a week. Over 100 rebels were arrested for treason and 90 were quickly condemned to death, including Pearse. However, an international outcry against this decision and the total lack of commonly accepted due process, caused the British to reduce the number condemned to 15. The executions were carried out by firing squad one month later in the yard of Kilmainham Gaol in Dublin. This inhumane action galvanized anti-British feelings among the Irish as few things had done in the past.

After the failure of the Easter Rising and the execution of the rebels, those who believed that only an armed revolution would accomplish their aims gained much more support. The years 1917 to 1921 were a period of violence administered by the IRB against British agents and military officials. The British responded by hiring mercenaries, known as the Black and Tans, who had been veterans of the war and were particularly vicious. The leaders of the Irish independence movement at this time were Eamon de Valera, Arthur Griffith, and Michael Collins. Collins was the head of the IRB and directed most of the attacks on British authority. De Valera and Griffith were the heads of the self-appointed secret and illegal Irish government.

In mid-1921, Lloyd George, still the Prime Minister, was determined to settle the "Irish problem" peacefully and consistent with the principle of self determination that had guided so much of the discussion in Paris two years earlier. The British government offered the Irish leaders a cessation of violence and a conference in London to discuss a "free state," something more than Home Rule but less than full independence. Griffith and Collins, to his considerable surprise, were appointed to attend the conference on behalf of Ireland.

The discussions lasted over two months but were never real negotiations. Lloyd George made clear that the British proposal was a "take it or leave it" proposition and if the Irish did not accept, the British would move many more troops into Ireland and force control. In essence, what was offered was a very broad Home Rule state which allowed an Irish Parliament to govern Ireland on virtually all matters except war, conscription, import-export protections for Britain, and loyalty to the crown. This latter point required an oath of loyalty to the King and was particularly troubling to many. However, the most controversial issue was the separation of six counties in Ulster to the north which would remain an integral part of Great Britain. This was done because of the presumed preference of a majority of the citizens of those counties. A vote in Ulster later confirmed this presumption. Griffith and Collins signed the agreement, known as the Anglo-Irish Treaty, on December 6, 1921 and returned to a land almost equally divided about its acceptance.

Even though the Irish legislature (the Dial) and a vote of the people confirmed the acceptance of the treaty, many were still opposed and were led by de Valera. Their primary opposition centered on the separation of Ulster from the rest of Ireland. A tragic civil war between the Irish, separating family members and friends on each side, ensued until May 24,

1923. The pro-treaty forces prevailed after much bloodshed. The Free State ultimately became the completely independent Republic of Ireland in 1937 with, ironically, de Valera, its strongest opponent in the beginning, as the Republic's first Prime Minister. A contentious division within Northern Ireland between Catholics and Protestants simmered for several decades until the 1970s, when terrorist activities were pursued by both sides. Finally, after several thousand pointless deaths, an agreement was reached between the opposing parties in Northern Ireland and endorsed by Britain on April 10, 1998. This "Good Friday Agreement" created a shared government and remains the basis of a tenuous peace today.

CHAPTER 4

The Russian Revolution and Fear of the Spread of Communism

Lenin and the Bolsheviks

AS NOTED ABOVE with regard to Ataturk and the Turkish Revolution, it is rare when one man can cast so long a shadow over so many millions of people and such a large land area, but such was also the case with Vladimir Lenin and his impact on Russia. The basic contours of the communist system fashioned by Lenin remained intact for about 70 years. Not only was he indispensable in bringing Bolshevism to power but he inspired and guided the organization of the communist movement, and he, more than anyone else, shaped the soviet system of rule during the first six years of its existence. *Soviet* means "councils of workers." Soviet leaders after Lenin's death in 1924 followed in detail the lines set down by the architect of the revolution. For over six decades soviet leaders considered Lenin's teachings to be sacrosanct and persistently invoked his name to justify their policies.

By January of 1917, Russia was effectively out of the war and labor strikes, poverty and famine were rampant all over the country. On March 10th, an estimated 200,000 people marched peacefully in St. Petersburg demanding bread and governmental reforms. The Tsar, who understood only autocratic rule, ordered his troops to fire on the demonstrators. Both officers and soldiers refused to do so, and the Tsar was forced to abdicate on March 15th. The leaders who remained formed a Provisional Government, but from the moment of its creation rival centers of authority challenged the government for control. The two principal groups were the Mensheviks and the Bolsheviks which had much in common but also important points of difference.

The Mensheviks consisted of a wide range of political parties, former officers of the imperial army, and nationalists who wished to secure independence. The Mensheviks believed the ultimate socialist revolution would be led by the bourgeois elements of society and not the proletariat workers. These groups were informally referred to as the "Whites."

The Bolsheviks were led by Lenin and an important revolutionary military leader, Leon Trotsky. Their group consisted mostly of workers, former soldiers and sailors, and peasants from the countryside. Like the Mensheviks, the Bolsheviks, commonly called "the Reds," were socialists, but unlike the Whites they were also devoted communists and followers of Marxist philosophy. In July of 1917, a spontaneous outpouring of people, estimated to be 500,000, demanded an end to the war and removal of the Provisional Government. Lenin was then in exile in Helsinki and unable to take advantage of the situation. He realized he had missed an opportunity and determined that that would not happen again. He returned in secret to Russia on October 10th. But now the Reds were much better organized with units of the Red Guard numbering over 25,000. On October 24th, the revolution was launched in St. Petersburg, and with virtually no resistance the Bolsheviks controlled the centers of power in the city. Lenin quickly announced a series of policies that he knew would be instantly popular. The most important was the land program transferring certain property rights from the nobility to the peasants. This was administered by a collection of Soviet Land Commissions. Land ownership remained with the state but peasants were given exclusive rights to farm the land, at least for the present.

However, Lenin did have to contend with growing political and military opposition to his regime in the beginning. From 1918 to late 1920 a brutal civil war raged in the country. By the spring of 1921, the Reds had defeated the Whites and had reestablished a semblance of order in most of what had been the Russian Empire. But there were important losses; Finland, Estonia, Latvia, Lithuania, and Poland all became independent states.

After the military victory, Lenin made it clear that he wanted autocratic powers, and he began that effort by suppressing newspapers and other forms of dissent. He also created a security police force with broad powers of arrest and even secret murders of opponents. The writing was clearly on the wall as to what was coming for the next four decades.

Economic reform was very high on the list of important governmental reforms both because of the philosophical tenets of communism but, more urgently, because of the disastrous state of the economy. In October of 1921, Lenin wisely backpedaled some on communist principles and explained his thinking in a statement on the first New Economic Policy (NEP): "Let us industrialize everything. Capitalists will be amongst us, foreign capitalists, concessionaires, and lease holders: they will wrest from us hundreds per cent of profit, they will flourish around us. Let them flourish; we will learn from them how to carry on industry, and then we shall be able to construct our Communist Republic." This level of pragmatism was necessary but, unfortunately for the Russian economy, was not followed very long because Lenin died early in 1924.

For four years the leaders of the Soviet Union (officially, the Union of Soviet Socialist Republics), violently struggled for power. This centered on a struggle between Trotsky and Joseph Stalin. It was not only a power struggle but an ideological one as well. Trotsky was true to Marx's principles of expanded revolution to bring communism to all industrialized countries. Stalin was more interested in consolidating control over Russia. Trotsky fully believed in Lenin's economic ideas of a minor level of capitalism within the NEP. Stalin viewed this as weakness. Stalin proved to be the more devious and secret manipulator of power centers, and by 1929 he had forced Trotsky and his supporters to leave Russia. Stalin arranged to have Trotsky murdered in Mexico on August 20, 1940. The Soviet Union under Stalin became totalitarian and the government sought to secure total control over national institutions and over people's affairs, private as well as public. No significant initiatives or policies were undertaken without the expressed approval of Stalin, the dictator.

Stalin—The Supreme Leader and the Great Purges

Stalin was born into a poor family in the border republic of Georgia and, unlike other early Bolshevik leaders, had not spent a long period in exile in other parts of Europe. He had much less education, was not intellectually inclined, and had no real internationalist leanings. However, he was very well organized, hard working, and brutal. He was even criticized by Lenin for excessive brutality, but Lenin did not dismiss him. Stalin became the Communist Party general secretary, a post that party intellectuals disdained and thought of as merely administrative. But his mastery of the position gave him exceptional power within the party to approve and disapprove of membership for lower level leaders.

The Soviet system had at least three interrelated centers of power that kept it functioning for about six decades: the Communist Party, the Secret Police and a system of incentives. Substantial rewards were given to loyal and energetic party members, especially those who rose to the upper reaches of the organization. They would receive faster promotions, more spacious apartments, attractive summer homes, admission for their children into the best schools, and other benefits.

Communist economic theory, as preached by Lenin and practiced by Stalin, involved a concept of a totally controlled economy with no opportunities for personal profits based on individual initiative. A good example of this is the collective farm. The government initiated a policy of collectivization of the agricultural sector meant to eliminate individual farms and merge them into large collective farms. The collectives were expected to be much more efficient than small private farms, and Soviet leaders planned to move the excess manpower to the cities. Huge numbers of Russian peasants resisted the authorities with every weapon at their disposal and class warfare spread across much of the countryside. During a two-year span from 1930 to 1931 approximately 400,000 households (roughly two million people) were forcibly deported from the countryside. The disruptions in the villages greatly reduced agricultural output and caused widespread famines.

The government did make some concessions to the peasants. They allowed some of them to have small private plots of land and to work both the collective farm and their own plots. Ironically, this two-fold arrangement demonstrated the effectiveness of economic incentives because the yields from the private land typically amounted to more than six times the yields of the collectives.

The management of state-owned industrial production moved much faster and more successfully than the agricultural collectivization. By the early 1930s, heavy industries such as iron, steel, tool making, electricity generating stations, and manufacturing facilities were expanding rapidly. Untrained workers from the countryside were becoming trained, or in some cases shipped out to distant work camps where the conditions were miserable. In spite of that, in a surprisingly short time the country could boast of having entirely new industries that produced tractors, automobiles, agricultural machinery, and airplanes.

Another aspect of Marxist philosophy that Stalin followed aggressively was Marx's attitude about religion. Marx famously said religion was the "opium of the people." Both Lenin and Stalin firmly agreed, and all religious practices were banned. This was not as difficult as we in the west might imagine because for centuries in Russia the Orthodox religious leaders had supported the tsar and the nobility. Between 1926 and 1937 the number of Orthodox priests in the Soviet Union decreased by half and the same was true, or worse, for Jewish rabbis, Catholic priests, Protestant ministers, and Muslim Imans. The clergy were not just removed but sometimes were arrested and even murdered. Churches were despoiled and turned into museums; schools and the press were exploited and forced to vilify religion.

The Stalinist purges of 1936 to 1938 undoubtedly marked the most infamous period in Soviet history. Hundreds of thousands of people were arrested for nothing more than suspicion of anti-revolutionary activity or writings. Mere association with those suspected was sufficient for long term imprisonment. No opportunity to defend oneself was offered, and many never returned from labor camps in Siberia.

Historians have questioned why Stalin engaged in such horrific slaughter of his own people, especially at this time when he was in such firm control. No definitive answer is available. It may well be that Stalin had become paranoid believing that everyone was a potential enemy and only by eliminating many could he be certain of including the few true threats. Moreover, the whole population would be so terrorized that no independent thought or action would again take place. A few statistics will reveal the scope of Stalin's war against his own military leaders. About half of the entire officer corps of the army, 35,000 men, were arrested; including 113 out of 115 army commanders, 220 out of 406 brigade commanders, and all eleven vice commissars of war. Some were executed immediately, and others were imprisoned for long periods in corrective labor camps, called *gulags*. By Stalin's death in March of 1953, the best estimates of the number of Russians eliminated in the Soviet Union during his term in power amounted to ten to twelve million people.

Having largely decimated his army leadership by 1938, Stalin now faced the most powerful military in Europe—Germany to the west. With war becoming a virtual certainty in the next year, he also correctly assumed that Britain and France would let the Soviets carry the major burden of defending against Germany. The Soviet Union needed time to prepare. Hitler also knew by mid-1939 that he would invade Poland, an action which likely would trigger the guarantees of protection Britain and France had agreed to provide to Poland through the Treaty of Versailles. While British and French defense of Poland was not a certainty, Hitler needed a nonaggression pact with the Soviets as much as Stalin needed one.

To the shock of the western world, on August 23, 1939, Hitler and Stalin announced an agreement that each would remain neutral in the event that the other was attacked. Hitler achieved his primary objective by ensuring a peaceful eastern border when war on the western front began. Stalin bought the time he needed to build up the military. It strains credulity to think that either of these unscrupulous dictators trusted the other, but the pact at least solved short term issues for each.

Every bit as important as the publicly disclosed aspects of the agreement, were the secret provisions in which the two countries agreed to divide Poland after the German invasion. Germany would regain Danzig and the western territories of Poland, while the Soviet Union would occupy the Baltic States and most of eastern Poland. The independent state of Poland would simply cease to exist.

Britain and France observed the Hitler-Stalin agreement with mixed feelings. Certainly the neutralization of the Soviets on Germany's eastern front was a very serious military problem for those fighting in the west. Furthermore, it was clear to everyone that the Russians could not put up a serious fight for at least two years in any event. On the other hand, the European capitalist countries were nearly as fearful of the rapid spread of communism from the Soviet Union. Stalin's brutal purges of the last few years were reasonably well known (perhaps not to their full extent) throughout Europe as well. Germany constituted the strongest bulwark against that threat. In 1939 there were still a few who believed that Hitler could be satisfied or, at least, mollified.

CHAPTER 5

The Rise of Fascism—Italy, Germany and Spain

Mussolini—Drive to Absolutism

T HE TERM *FASCISM* is frequently used to describe a number of right-wing dictatorships, but the word derives from *Fasci di combattimento* meaning "Bands of Combat." It was used as the name of an Italian political party started in 1919 and composed largely of war veterans and workers. It was also a political philosophy that encompassed anti-democracy, anti-Marxism, and often anti-Semitism. The fascist governments were usually single party dictatorships characterized by terrorism and police surveillance. These movements also championed the cult of a great leader.

Benito Mussolini (1883-1945) was an opportunist of the first order. He could change his ideas and principles to suit every new occasion. Action for him was always more important than thought or rational justification. In his early career, Mussolini was a socialist, and he formed a newspaper with a strong leftist leaning. It was called *Il Popolo d'Italia (The People of Italy),* but later he discovered that many upper and middle class Italians feared the loss of their property and had no sympathy for socialism or the workers that it protected. They wanted order. As a result, Mussolini changed his philosophy, adopted fascism, and took direct action in the face of government inaction.

By 1920 the Italian Fascists were determined to crush the socialists. They formed local squads of terrorists who disrupted Socialist Party meetings, and beat up their leaders and supporters. Conservative landowners and businessmen were grateful. Fascism, despite being still highly local in its base and organization, began to exhibit the first signs of a national appeal and purpose. Two years later, the Fascists expanded their intimidation to local government officials in northern cities, especially Milan. By October, Mussolini could count hundreds of thousands of supporters, and he led them on a peaceful march on Rome. King Victor Emmanuel III refused to authorize the army to stop the marchers and within weeks asked Mussolini to become Prime Minister. On November 23, 1922, the King and Parliament granted Mussolini dictatorial authority for one year to bring order to local and regional government.

Always a concern in Italian politics was the influence of the Vatican. The Church, while holding no real power, did have significant influence over various segments of Italian society. The Fascist movement benefited by the death in January 1922 of Pope Benedict XV who had opposed all oppressive regimes, especially the Fascists and the Bolsheviks. He was succeeded by the Archbishop of Milan who took the name Pius XI. Mussolini and his northern associates immediately did their best to ingratiate themselves with the new Pope. This paid dividends later in 1929 when the Lateran Treaty between Mussolini's government and the Vatican was signed. It recognized the Vatican as a sovereign state and guaranteed non-interference by the Church in Italian governmental matters. It brought Mussolini badly needed respect and silence about his authoritarian regime. The Treaty was later used as a model in other countries, including Germany.

By 1926, all political parties other than the Fascists were dissolved and Mussolini transformed Italy into a dictatorial state. Many respectable Italians tolerated and even admired Mussolini because they believed he had saved them from Bolshevism. Another area of importance was the suppression of the press. Established independent Roman newspapers were falsely accused of encouraging two assassination attempts on Mussolini. There has always been some doubt about the second; it may well have been staged. These newspapers were closed down and their property was destroyed. Then, very cleverly, the Fascists closed all newspapers but offered to allow them to reopen with generous government loans, if they would toe the line. They all did, and the government had a loyal press.

No sooner had Mussolini achieved unquestioned autocratic powers, neutralized the Vatican, and silenced the press than he faced an international problem that he could not resolve. The economic depression of the 1930s affected all industrialized countries, including Italy. Virtually all European countries were deeply in debt with most loans being held by United States lenders. When the American stock exchange declined precipitously at the end of 1929, European loans were called in and many defaulted, thus exacerbating the problem on both sides of the Atlantic. However, the Italian government was better prepared than most because Mussolini had created a planned economy that linked private ownership of capital to government arbitration of labor disputes. Major industries were organized into syndicates and the government had a strong influence over the kind and quantity of production. This corporate state allowed the government to direct much of the nation's economic life without a formal change of ownership. Later, in 1935, Mussolini attacked and occupied Ethiopia, further justifying placing the country on a wartime economy with even tighter governmental controls.

Hitler—Rise to Power and Pre-War Developments

In Germany in the early 1920s, inflation was destroying society and the standard of living to which most Germans had grown accustomed. One American dollar was worth approximately 800 million German marks. In other words, German currency was worthless. Late in 1923 Adolf Hitler (1889-1945) made his first major appearance on the German political scene. Hitler absorbed much of the rabid German nationalism, racism, and extreme anti-Semitism that flourished in Vienna, Austria, where he lived at that time. His party became known as The National Socialist German Workers Party, simply known as the Nazis. The party platform called for repudiation of the Versailles Treaty, the unification of Austria and Germany, and the exclusion of Jews from German citizenship. The word "socialism" in the party's name was a sham. Because of the economic depression, the extreme political parties, especially the Nazis, gained considerable support among war veterans and unemployed workers who experienced economic and social displacement.

As Hitler established his dominance in the Nazi Party, he clearly had the model of Mussolini in mind and spoke of the Italian dictator's accomplishments in glowing terms. On November 9, 1923, Hitler and a band of followers attempted a *putsch* (sudden political revolt) from a beer hall in Munich. When the local authorities crushed the attempted uprising, Hitler and others were arrested and tried for treason. Although Hitler used the trial to make himself into a national figure, he was convicted and sentenced to five years in prison. He was paroled after serving only a few months. During his time in prison, Hitler wrote *Mein Kampf* (My Struggle) where he outlined key political views including fierce anti-Semitism, opposition to Bolshevism, and a conviction that Germany must expand eastward into Poland and Ukraine. Thus, those Germans who professed later to be unaware of Hitler's intentions and ultimate direction were clearly either extremely uninformed or attempting to justify their complaisance.

Hitler's rise to power was far more complicated and took much longer than Mussolini's but was no less absolute in achieving dictatorial powers. The German government of the 1920s consisted of a parliament, called the *Reichstag*, which was fairly weak, a president, Field Marshall Paul von Hindenburg, (a General in World War I), and a chancellor appointed by the president who, like a prime minister, held most of the powers. As previously noted, the decade of the 1920s was extremely difficult economically for Germany, and the government, known as the Weimar Republic, had little success in improving the economy. In fact by 1932, German unemployment had risen to over six million, mostly among youths, with no improvement in sight. The Nazis held mass rallies and gained powerful supporters in business, the military, and publishing circles.

President von Hindenburg, at the age of 83, announced in 1932 that he would run again for president. Hitler's goal was not the presidency but the chancellorship, where the real power resided. He knew though that Hindenburg would not appoint him chancellor and, in fact, had negative personal views toward Hitler. He often referred to him as the "house painter." Hitler was persuaded by his followers to oppose Hindenburg and run for president. Although he lost the election, he received 30% of the vote in the first balloting and 37% in the runoff election. The Nazi Party won 230 seats in the Reichstag, which amounted to the largest voting block in the legislature. Hitler demanded to be appointed chancellor. Hindenburg refused and appointed Franz von Papen, a weak and extremely conservative associate of the President. Hitler was privately offered the vice-chancellorship but he refused. Hitler informed the President's representatives that he had dedicated himself to wiping out the Marxist parties and that this could not be done unless he took over the government and ran things his own way. He added that one could not shy away from bloodshed and asked, mockingly, if the King of Italy had offered Mussolini the vice-chancellorship after the march on Rome. There were several conversations directly between Hindenburg and Hitler, but neither would budge from his position. Hindenburg was finding it impossible to form a government without the participation of the Nazis. He was also being besieged by supporters among the finance, industrial, and military establishments to appoint Hitler as chancellor. They saw in Hitler order, economic development, and strong resistance to communism. The final straw for Hindenburg was when Hitler demanded new elections to determine who would be chancellor. He very reluctantly appointed Hitler as chancellor on January 30, 1933.

Once in office, Hitler moved rapidly to consolidate his control. This process involved three steps: the capture of full legal authority, the crushing of alternative political groups, and the purging of rivals within the Nazi party itself. By March of 1933, the Reichstag passed an Enabling Act that permitted Hitler to rule by decree. A few months later, in June and July, all other German political parties were outlawed, and the Nazis were now the only legal party in Germany and Hitler was their unchallenged leader.

Although publicly unchallenged, Hitler was still concerned about secret cabals against his leadership, particularly in the SA, a paramilitary organization within the Nazi party. The SA, also known as the *brownshirts,* was headed by Ernst Roehm, a former military officer who had supported Hitler from the beginning. Roehm wanted to have control, or at least parity, with the formal German military who, of course, strongly resisted any such concepts. Hindenburg was still a revered figure among the military, and Hitler did not want further confrontations with the President. Hitler knew that any long term control of the country would require the full support of the German army. It has never been clear that Roehm led a conspiracy against Hitler, but some high elements of the SA were certainly resisting party direction. After much internal consternation, Hitler agreed with his principal advisors to move against the SA leadership, and in one weekend of June 30-July 2, 1934 rounded up more than 200 SA leaders and others suspected of collaboration, including Roehm. Approximately 100 were executed, along with Roehm, who professed his loyalty to Hitler to the end. One month later, President Hindenburg died of natural causes, and Hitler had the Reichstag combine the offices of president and chancellor. He now held dictatorial power over all of Germany including the Wehrmacht, the combined military forces. Later, all members of the military were required to make pledges of loyalty, not just to the country but to Adolf Hitler personally.

By the mid-1930s, the German economy had recovered dramatically. The reasons were twofold: its industrial base had not been damaged during the first war, and Hitler's government was embarked on a huge military buildup, increasingly in violation of the Versailles Treaty. This should not have been a surprise to anyone since Hitler had long ago expressed his intention not to honor the Treaty, especially the military rebuilding restrictions. German militarization moved faster and faster as Hitler tested the will of the French and British to restrain it. Both governments were found to be unwilling to take any action. One exception to this was Winston Churchill who warned often that Hitler could not be trusted

Also during this time, the anti-Semitism of the Nazis and other Germans became increasingly virulent. In 1933 Jews were prohibited from all civil service, and in 1935 they were robbed of their citizenship. Jewish owned businesses were being harassed and in some cases confiscated. This was happening in plain sight but with no significant complaint from either the German people or the various Christian churches. On November 9-10 of 1938, Hitler and the Nazis showed the true colors of their racial prejudice when Jewish stores and synagogues were burned and otherwise destroyed in what is known as *Kristallnacht* ("Crystal Night").

On the international scene, Hitler followed a process he used in the political and economic arenas by taking small steps initially but never backing down or wavering from his stated goals. One of these involved the Rhineland, which was part of Germany on the border with France but west of the Rhine river. The Versailles Treaty allowed Germany to retain this land but required that it be a demilitarized zone. Hitler simply sent troops to occupy the Rhineland in 1936 and, although the French complained, they did nothing about it. Next Hitler demanded the return of the Sudetenland, an area previously part of Germany but awarded to Czechoslovakia under the terms of the Treaty. The Czechs objected and requested assistance from France and Britain. A conference in Munich was held in September of 1938. It was attended by Neville Chamberlain of Britain, Edouard Daladier of France, Italian representatives, and Hitler, but not the Czechs. The British and French gave in completely to Hitler and only obtained his promise that he had no further territorial claims. Chamberlain returned to England and proclaimed they had achieved "peace in our time." The term *appeasement* has ever since been associated with this agreement.

But the following year, 1939, demonstrated even more dramatic Nazi demands. Hitler capitalized further on the German anger about decisions made by the Allied leaders in Paris in 1919, specifically the loss of the German city, Danzig, in the east Prussian area. The Treaty changed the city into a free port city with unrestricted access from the Baltic to the reestablished independent Poland. The vast majority of German citizens supported the reinstatement of Danzig as an integral part of Germany. It wasn't long after the agreement at Munich in September 1938 that Hitler began demanding that Danzig and the whole transportation corridor south to Poland be placed under exclusive German control. The Poles vigorously opposed any change and demanded support from Britain and France. However, German military forces in 1939 had been virtually restored to their levels before World War I, so Hitler was determined, at some point soon, to occupy Danzig and invade Poland.

But there were many uncertainties. Perhaps first and foremost was the reaction of Stalin and the Soviet Union to German troops at or near the Russians' western border. This issue was considered in chapter 4, primarily from the Soviet point of view, but Hitler had serious concerns as well. Ever since the days of Bismarck in the previous century, German leaders had been worried about a two front war. Of course, this is exactly what happened in World War I. Consequently, Hitler promoted a very quick, non-aggression pact with Stalin that was signed on August 23, 1939. The basic terms were previously covered, but from Hitler's viewpoint, it guaranteed no military resistance from the Soviets when he invaded Poland.

Hitler was still convinced, because of the opinions of his foreign policy advisors, that Britain and France would not wage a large European war to save Poland. So with his east protected and an unjustified optimism about the western powers, Germany invaded Poland on September 1, 1939. Two days later Britain and France declared war and World War II had begun.

Spanish Fascism and Civil War

If one were to draw sides as a prelude to the next great war, one could hardly do better than to consider the Spanish Civil War which broke out in 1936. As the war in Spain advanced in the next two years, the Allied powers, Russia and France, sided with the incumbent socialist/communist government, while Germany and Italy sided with the revolutionary fascists under General Francisco Franco. But Spain was different from all the other western European powers because it had remained neutral during World War I and, therefore, was in much better condition economically. It profited from extensive international markets which encouraged its business leaders to push for more capitalist reforms, improve conditions of the working class, and reduce the dominance of the agrarian sector.

The first Republic had been declared in 1931 after King George was forced into exile because of his resistance to any change seen by many to be necessary to modernize the country. The new government consisted of an odd combination of liberal republicans, socialists, intellectuals, and nationalists who wanted greater local autonomy. One thing that united these disparate groups was aggressive anticlerical legislation. The Catholic Church in Spain had for centuries associated itself with reactionary forces of the old regime, especially the monarchy, and opposed all liberalism and modernization. The governments that followed implemented many reforms both democratic and economic, but could not unify the plethora of parties that were active. When national elections were held in February 1936, a new group called the Spanish Popular Front won most positions in the government. This party was made up of leftists, communists, and anarchists. This was too much for the conservative military leaders who lacked only a strong leader and admired the models of totalitarian fascism in Italy and Germany. General Franco filled that void quickly and formed an army in Spanish Morocco in the south, across from Gibraltar. In July his army, known generally as the "Fascists," began to move north through the center of Spain with a goal to take Madrid rapidly. That did not happen.

As mentioned above, Franco was supported by Hitler and Mussolini's fascist governments with weapons, artillery, and even tanks and airplanes. In some cases the planes were piloted by German pilots. The Popular Front government was initially supported by the Soviet Union and later by France but never to the extent supplied by the Axis powers. The Civil War took on a romantic aura because of the stark ideological contrasts between liberal and conservative economic and political models. Socialism and communism were far more popular in the mid 1930s than today, and many western ideologues, like Ernest Hemingway, came to Spain to volunteer to help the elected Popular Front government.

France had the most to lose from a Franco victory because it would place hostile fascist powers to its south as well as its east. However, ironically, France did very little practically to assist the leftist government. Even as late as the second half of the 1930s, there was still nearly as much fear of the spread of communism from Russia as there was fear of Nazi Germany. These dual fears had the effect of paralyzing government decision making and giving rise to unwarranted optimism and appeasement. The British were also not of one mind regarding Franco; did he represent a threat or a protection of British interests? British diplomatic correspondence in July of 1936 stated one view: "Everyone anxiously awaits result of General Franco's *coup d'etat*. Should he fail, I believe dangerous disorders are bound to occur in (Spain)." (Consul Harold Patteson)

In an effort to localize the conflict in Spain, the British, French, and US governments urged all interested countries to informally join a Non-Intervention agreement, pledging not to arm or otherwise assist either side in the Civil War. Germany and Italy immediately agreed and then continued their support of Franco. The Soviets, at least, did not play the sham, ignoring the non-intervention effort and continuing their support of the Popular Front government. Stalin was having some success in organizing the International Brigades, who were foreign fighters committed to leftist causes in several countries and who enthusiastically came to Spain to fight the fascists. This international involvement was consistent with Marxist principles of the spread of communism around the developed world and, of course, reinforced the opinions of those whose greatest fear was the communist movement.

Most observers of the war in late 1936 fully expected Franco to take control of Madrid by the end of the year. However, after fierce fighting and much destruction in the City, the Popular Front and their leftist supporters held out, and Franco ended the assault of the city on November 22nd. Franco then split his army moving one group northeast to reach the Mediterranean about 100 miles south of Barcelona, and the other group advanced north to reach the Basque area on the French border. By now it was clear that the Fascists could not be defeated, and even a long holdout by the Popular Front would require far greater support from outside sources.

However, in early 1938, the attention of all of Europe was focused on the Nazi threat, and very few leaders concerned themselves with Spain. The respected American historian, Philip Minehan, has described the atmosphere in Europe at this time: "The drive behind the firm Nazi and Italian Fascist commitment to a Spanish rebel victory was, first of all, part of the pan-European momentum of fascism on the offensive, spurred on by the appeasement of it by the liberal democracies led by Great Britain. The recklessly experimental and aggressively expansionistic characters of the Third Reich and Fascist Italy required dramatic political-military successes both for their domestic and international prestige and fearsomeness."

Perhaps capitalizing on this reduced attention, Franco aggressively and brutally attacked city after city until in January 1939 Barcelona fell and Franco consolidated his armies for a second attack on Madrid. The capital City was taken with no resistance on March 27th. Four days later Franco announced, "Today, with the Red Army captive and disarmed . . . the war is over." Final numbers of dead, wounded, and displaced in this three-year civil war have never really been available, but informed estimates suggest several hundred thousand. When the second World War began, Spain quickly announced its neutrality but secretly helped Germany with intelligence and other important assistance.

More recently, since the 1960s, there have been significant liberalizations and economic development and a return to a constitutional monarchy. During Franco's rule these changes decisively reduced his dictatorial powers and strengthened his opposition. Moreover, the Catholic Church functioned more freely after Vatican II and saw an increase in younger clergy. Later, Spain entered the European Union and in 2002 adopted the euro as its currency. (More about this in a later chapter.)

CHAPTER 6

World War II—European Theater

Early Actions of the Nazis

AFTER THE WESTERN powers were intimidated by Hitler at Munich in September of 1938, he became increasingly convinced that they were mostly words and not action. His primary goal in 1939 was the absorption back into Germany of the City of Danzig and the elimination of the Polish corridor. Once Hitler accomplished his non-aggression pact with Stalin, he felt no restraint in moving against Poland. Essentially, this agreement doomed Poland because the Soviets, in effect, agreed not to intervene if Germany attacked Poland. On September 1, 1939, the Nazis did just that. In a matter of a few weeks, the Germans had taken control of most of Poland and the City of Danzig. They then began to divide up certain territories for the Soviets, including Estonia, Lithuania, and Latvia on the Baltic, and parts of Poland bordering the Soviet Union. On September 3, 1939, Britain and France surprised Hitler by declaring war on Germany and World War II began.

The early months of the war in the west saw complete German victories in Denmark, Netherlands, and a little later, Belgium. Their success in Norway, however, was not so fast or easy. Norway was a strategically important country for Germany because it offered protection to the "Homeland" from the north and provided excellent deep water ports on the North Sea for German warships to move out into the Atlantic. An important disadvantage was that it was close (about 400 miles) from the main British naval base at Scapa Flow, Scotland. From the earliest days of the war the superior British Navy constantly patrolled and dominated the North Sea.

The British, in their own interest, were quick to assist the Norwegians, even sending troops to invade the northwestern part of the country. But the Germans had succeeded in occupying the more populous and important south, including Oslo. Numerous skirmishes occurred making it clear to most observers that British troops were not properly led, trained, or equipped. There were, however, several fierce naval battles between German and British destroyers off the Norwegian coast. Two capital ships, the German cruiser *Blucher* and the British carrier *Glorious,* were both sunk with the loss of nearly 1,000 on each side. The British eventually withdrew and the Nazis occupied Norway to nearly the end of the war. During the fighting the Germans lost about 5,300 to the British losses of 4,500.

Although Finland was never a part of the German-Soviet pact, Stalin saw this as an opportune time to move against the lightly populated land to the north. Helsinki was only a short distance across the Baltic from Leningrad and would have been an excellent point from which to attack, if occupied by a hostile government. Finland also had large sources of nickel so necessary in arms manufacture. In October of 1939, Stalin demanded complete control of all important areas of Finland, but the Finns immediately rejected the demands. Stalin believed no tiny population of 3.6 million could possibly resist the huge Soviet Union. But the Finns were a very proud people and relished their independence. A local joke at the time expressed the spirit of the people: "They (Russian troops) are so many and our country is so small, where shall we find room to bury them all."

Finland is mountainous with narrow, often snow-covered primitive passageways. Although the Soviets had tanks and motorized vehicles, they were constantly attacked from high positions, often with light, easily transported weapons such as machine guns and gasoline bombs. The Soviets made advances into Finland but always at great cost in personnel and equipment. One assault in January 1940 received attention and much praise in the west. The Russians attacked with 4,000 troops against only 32 well positioned Finns. The Russians prevailed but lost 400 men to 28 Finns. The Finnish army occasionally counterattacked, but their victories were short-lived. The war ground on in 1940 without significant change until the Soviets realized later in the year that a far greater menace was building on their western border. Stalin's co-conspirator in aggression was moving millions of soldiers and equipment east to the Russian border.

The battle for France began in earnest in the spring of 1940. Once his northern border was protected with the defeat of Norway, Hitler advanced his *Wehrmacht* (defense force) quickly on a long front into France. The French relied on the so called "Maginot Line" which was a defense line of heavy fortifications reminiscent of World War I trenches. The French military leadership was also burdened with concepts and plans long out-dated and which had been none too successful in the last war.

The mechanized German army moved very quickly, penetrating the defenses and capturing hundreds of thousands of French troops from behind. For the most part, it was not a case, as some historians have alleged, of French soldiers' reluctance to fight but a total failure of modern military competence by the French generals. The fastest German movement was in the north through Belgium and then a straight line to Paris. (The Schlieffen Plan?) By June of 1940 the German occupation of all of northern France, including Paris, was inevitable, and the French government decided to surrender rather than to see its beloved city destroyed. The Germans allowed a collaborator government to be established in the south of France with a capital at Vichy. This area was known as Vichy France and was completely subordinate to Hitler.

Prior to total German occupation, the British arranged a courageous removal of their soldiers and many thousands of French soldiers from the Belgian port of Dunkirk. This was accomplished under heavy air attack from the German air force and with the brave volunteer assistance of many small boat owners from Dover across the Channel. It is estimated that in three days of crossings, about 350,000 soldiers were saved to fight another day.

During the winter of 1940 and spring of 1941 the Germans launched air attacks almost daily on Great Britain, and especially London. However, the British resisted at great cost and ultimately stopped Hitler in what is known as the *Battle of Britain*. The Royal Air Force (RAF) defended the home island courageously and destroyed nearly twice as many planes of the Luftwaffe as the RAF lost. After nearly a year of German bombing attacks, Hitler finally became convinced that he could not subdue Britain through air attacks alone.

Continental Europe was under almost total domination of Germany and Italy until the summer of 1941 when Hitler, flush with victory, breached his agreement with Stalin and invaded the Soviet Union. Many observers have questioned why Hitler chose to attack the Soviets at this time since he was still fighting Britain in the west and Stalin presented no immediate threat to Germany. In retrospect, the decision was a bad one, but after virtually no resistance anywhere in Europe, Hitler believed his Wehrmacht, and more importantly he himself, were invincible. In addition, he observed the great difficulties Stalin had in subduing tiny Finland and concluded that the Soviet Union was a paper tiger. He also knew that Stalin was on a crash course to rebuild his military forces and that waiting probably meant a tougher fight for the Nazis. In any event, *Operation Barbarossa* was launched on June 22, 1941. As Hitler expected, the attack completely surprised Stalin and the German army advanced quickly and deeply into Russia. They reached Leningrad (current St. Petersburg) and the outskirts of Moscow in November. The Germans were able to capture huge numbers of Russian troops, roughly 2.5 million, because of advanced planning by the Germans and virtually no planning by the Soviets.

However, the tide turned at the end of the year when the Russian winter, which had so devastated Napoleon in the 19th century and stalled the German army in the prior war, set in. The Nazis were woefully unprepared because they expected to occupy Moscow before winter and, at least psychologically, to end resistance on their eastern front. Hitler delayed a final seizure of the capital city and moved many divisions to the south to capture important oil facilities. With a reprieve of a few months, Stalin reinforced defenses and began to attack German supply lines that were stretched to breaking. The light, fast German mechanized army became mired in mud and snow and was an easy target. The Germans retreated to defensive positions and resolved to renew the attack in the spring.

But another important development occurred at the end of 1941 that changed the whole complexion of the war. The United States declared war on Japan after that nation's attack at Pearl Harbor in the Hawaiian Islands. Within a few days, Germany and the US had exchanged declarations of war, and now Britain was no longer alone in the western front but had an exceptionally powerful, if unprepared, ally in their struggle with Hitler.

American Entry and Final Defeat of Germany

Churchill and his countrymen were certainly happy to have the US with them, at last, to buttress their cause, now in its third year. However, the British soon realized that they were required to give up some elements of control, both military and political. Fortunately, the political leadership of the two countries, Prime Minister Winston Churchill and President Franklin Roosevelt, had an excellent relationship and had actually met on several occasions before the US entry into the war. Directions were given on both sides for full cooperation in military planning and operation. No joint command on such a large scale in a world war had ever been attempted before, and there was certainly no guarantee that this one would succeed. The top military commanders, US General George Marshall and British General Alan Brooke, had a frosty relationship at first, but both eventually came to respect each other and insist that their subordinates cooperate completely.

One early military planning issue that divided the Allies was that of when and where to launch the combined attack on continental Europe. After much discussion, it was agreed that the US would not be ready for such a massive undertaking until 1943. The great difference of opinion about where to attack was a sustained dividing point between the Allies. US planners wanted the invasion to be at the heart of Germany, landing across the Channel in France and moving quickly to the industrial Ruhr Valley in northwest Germany. British planners, actually led by Churchill himself, believed that the German defenses in France were much too formidable and it was wiser to attack the "soft underbelly" in the south—Sicily and Italy. Both positions had merit, but the final determinant was that by the spring of 1943, the US would not have been prepared either with equipment or personnel to launch the attack that it wanted. However, some action was necessary soon to show the home front and the enemy the determination and fighting spirit of the Allies.

In November of 1942, British and US troops launched attacks from the east and the west on German forces in North Africa. The British held Egypt in the east and in October moved west against the Afrika Korps under General Erwin Rommel. Both British and American forces landed at Vichy French Algeria and Morroco in November. The fighting was slow and difficult, but German supplies were nearly cut off by Allied air dominance. The Afrika Korps was defeated in some of the most famous tank battles in history. The Germans ultimately surrendered in May of 1943. This provided an opportunity for the Allies to attack from the south into Italy. At the same time the Russians were holding the German advance at great loss to themselves as well as to the Germans, particularly during the battle of Stalingrad, where Hitler lost over 800,000 troops by death, illness and capture.

British and American forces invaded Sicily in August 1943 and after some resistance moved on to Italy. The fighting and terrain in Italy were exceptionally challenging, and the Allied advance was slowed to a few miles per day. The German army had basically taken over the defense of Italy from the inept Italians. Indeed, Mussolini was thrown out of power in July, and after hiding out for nearly two years was unceremoniously executed in April of 1945. The fighting in Italy continued until nearly the end of the war but had the benefit to the Allies of tying up many German divisions that were not then available at Normandy in 1944.

By 1943 the British and the Americans dominated the air and launched devastating attacks on Germany causing the destruction of many

ARTHUR DREA

German cities, including Cologne, Dresden, and eventually Berlin. The Allies launched "D-Day" on June 6, 1944 by invading the French coast at Normandy. After less than one additional year, the Allies and the Russians defeated the Nazis, who surrendered in May of 1945.

There were many devastating effects of the European portion of the war, but undoubtedly the most horrific was Hitler's "Final Solution" of the Jewish population in Germany, and all the occupied countries. The systematic mass murder, known as the "Holocaust," massacred more than 6 million Jews and other opponents of Hitler in less than seven years. Anti-Semitism was rampant in many parts of Europe before the war, and Hitler succeeded in his racist dementia by unjustly blaming the Jews for virtually all of the problems of Germany in the 1920s and 1930s.

Britain, American and Soviet Discussions

Even before the war was over, Churchill, Roosevelt and Stalin were holding discussions about post-war matters. They were determined not to repeat the mistakes made in Paris in 1919. Churchill and Roosevelt were mostly concerned with Stalin's control of eastern Europe. An important conference between the big three was held in early February 1945 at Yalta in the Crimea. There, important decisions were reached, which essentially allowed the Soviet Union to dominate all of eastern Europe and half of Germany, including Berlin. The Allies were to control the western half of Germany and certain sections of the City of Berlin. It was clear that Stalin would have resisted, to the point of war, any agreement requiring the Soviet Union to give up control of the territories it had conquered. The Allies were unwilling to continue a massive war against a now very powerful adversary, the Soviet Union.

Clouding some of the discussions was the attitude of Churchill on the need to preserve the British colonies as they had been prior to the war. This view was not shared by Roosevelt, and needless to say, not by Stalin either. At an earlier conference (Tehran, Nov. 1944), Churchill expressed his opinions in characteristically clear terms when he stated that as far as Britain was concerned it did not desire to acquire any new territory or bases, but intended to hold on to what it had. He said that nothing would be taken from England without a war. He mentioned specifically Singapore and Hong Kong. Of course, things changed significantly after the war with India becoming independent in 1947, Singapore in 1965, and Hong Kong in 1997.

After the war many types of inventories were taken, but the one statistical fact that shocked the world and many Europeans especially, was the massive production of war materiel generated in a relatively short time by the United States. The US had produced, starting in 1942, more airplanes, ships, tanks, motorized vehicles, bombs, small arms, ammunition, and other materiel than all other combatant countries on both sides combined. One example is worth mentioning: during the war years the US produced 8,812 major naval vessels, while Britain, Germany, the Soviet Union, Italy, and Japan together produced 3,187. Obviously, the ability of the Allies to quickly replace damaged materiel, often with superior new equipment, was a huge advantage.

CHAPTER 7

Soviet Threat and NATO

The Emergence of American Influence in Europe

F OR OVER A century and a half, most Americans believed their government should heed the words of George Washington as he left the presidency, "Beware of foreign entanglements." By this he meant to avoid treaties and other commitments that could bring the US into war. That advice was followed for the most part until the end of the Second World War when it changed dramatically. Isolationism was dead as a foreign policy and the US had to become a world leader, whether that was a popular policy or not.

During the winter of 1946-47, the worst in memory, Europe seemed on the verge of collapse. In London, coal shortages left only enough fuel to heat and light homes for a few hours a day. In Berlin, the vanquished were freezing and starving to death. European cities were seas of rubble, 500 million cubic yards of it in Germany alone.

In America small groups of individuals, led by George C. Marshall, the Secretary of State, were organizing a relief effort to assist all of western Europe. The European Recovery Program, better known as the "Marshall Plan," was an extraordinary act of strategic generosity. It amounted to over $100 billion in today's values or about six times what America now spends on foreign aid. The relief got underway in June of 1947 and, according to former Prime Minster Winston Churchill, the Marshall Plan was: "the most unsordid act in history." Marshall's name was connected with it because of his unequalled reputation as the US military's highest-ranking general in the war, referred to by many as the "organizer of victory." Marshall explained the Plan as: "Our policy is not directed against any country or doctrine, but against hunger, poverty, desperation and chaos." By 1948 there were 150 ships per day carrying food and fuel to Europe, and the result was a constant rise in Europe's per capita GNP during the years 1948-51. The Plan also helped America by staving off communism in western Europe.

In the West some countries, such as France and Italy, were reestablishing democratic republics and containing communism as minority political parties. The Soviet Union offered a marked contrast, however. The eastern European countries within the Soviet sphere were governed autocratically through puppet governments controlled from Moscow. The two sides represented two fundamentally different world views: one upheld the principles of free enterprise, personal freedom, and popular participation in government. The other upheld one party rule, public ownership of the means of production, state control over all institutions, and economic and social rigidity. This bitter conflict between the communist and capitalist worlds was commonly referred to as the "cold war," but it was confined to economic, political and military development rivalries, and not actual war. This contrast was never more evident than in the post war divided Germany. The victors agreed to divide Germany roughly in half between east and west. West Germany was controlled by Britain, France and the United States, and East Germany was dominated by the Soviets. Berlin, being well within the Soviet sector, was also divided nearly in half between east and west. Stalin initially agreed to allow access from the west to Berlin through East Germany. Because of the harshness of Soviet control, ordinary German citizens began to migrate in large numbers from the east to the west. This was especially true in Berlin. To make movement more difficult and to punish West Berliners for their apparent disloyalty, Stalin breached his agreement in June of 1948 and cut off all access to West Berlin from the Allied sectors. The British and Americans responded by supplying West Berlin with essentials such as food, medicine, and fuel by air. Although difficult, this airlift basically broke the Soviet blockade and Stalin lifted it in May of 1949.

While the west was rebuilding in the late 1940s, the Soviet Union was embarking on an economic policy similar to that of its pre-war pattern. The emphasis was on heavy industry to the neglect of consumer goods. The battle cry was to overtake the west in economic production and to produce as quickly as possible an atom bomb. Under intense pressure from Stalin and by stealing nuclear secrets from the US and Britain, the Soviets were able to successfully explode an atom bomb in August 1949. For the next forty years the world would be dominated by two superpowers with nuclear weapons capable of mutual annihilation.

Immediately after the war, the United States developed a foreign policy known as "containment". Also called the Truman Doctrine, it emphasized resistance to Soviet expansion with the expectation that the Soviet Union would collapse from internal economic pressures and the burdens of its

ARTHUR DREA

foreign oppression. The United States undertook enormous military expenditures and sent large amounts of money abroad. However, the Soviets maintained their dominance over eastern Europe and East Germany and ultimately built a wall across eastern Europe to prohibit citizens of those countries from escaping.

The North Atlantic Treaty Organization (NATO) was created in April of 1949 and consisted of Italy, Denmark, Norway, Portugal, Canada and the United States. Later France, Britain, West Germany, Greece and Turkey joined NATO. Its purpose was to establish a commitment between its members to provide mutual assistance, including military assistance if necessary, in the event any member was attacked. As a charter member, the US offered the strongest element of defense to the other members, and for the first time in the nation's history, it had agreed to a major mutual defense treaty. It is consistent with the Truman Doctrine of containment in that it did not threaten action against the Soviet Union unless the Soviets first moved to expand their territory in Europe. The Soviets attempted to counter NATO by creating in May of 1955 their own mutual defense agreement called the "Warsaw Pact." Besides the USSR the Pact included Albania, Bulgaria, Czechoslovakia, East Germany, Hungary, Poland, and Romania—all nations under the thumb of the Soviets.

One country originally included in the Soviet sphere after the war could not be included in the Warsaw Pact, Yugoslavia. The Yugoslav communist regime was controlled by Josip Broz Tito, a universally respected war leader who had challenged Nazi occupation and commanded great popular prestige. Large numbers of Yugoslavs of all backgrounds were proud of his resistance and many successes against the occupiers. After the war, Tito moved quickly to consolidate several small countries (Soviet style) into one Yugoslavia and under his total control. Initially Stalin tried to dominate Tito, but Tito refused to follow the out-dated and failed economic policies of Stalinization. Specifically, he refused to implement agrarian collectivization as directed by Moscow. There were other important differences and, in 1948, Tito led Yugoslavia out of the Soviet Union. Stalin was faced with a serious challenge for the first time from a satellite country. There were several reasons why Stalin did not wish to send the Red Army into Yugoslavia: Tito and his government had been established by the Yugoslavs themselves and not by the Soviets; Tito was a committed communist, and total loyalty from the Russian Army to move against him was problematic; Tito presented no threat to the Soviets or any of his neighbors; and military domination of Yugoslavia would be very difficult and costly, as the Germans had discovered.

Post Stalin Soviet Union

When on March 5, 1953, the feared and despised Stalin died, some optimistic leaders in the west expected great changes to occur. They were to be disappointed. Nikita Khrushchev was appointed Party Secretary immediately, but the Politburo, the Soviet governing body, was slow to bestow absolute power on any one person. However, Khrushchev maneuvered himself into the Premiership three years later. It was clear then that he was in complete control when he made a secret speech to the Party Congress denouncing the crimes of Stalin in the strongest terms, calling him an enemy of the people. It is not certain if Khrushchev really intended that the speech be kept secret, but in fact, it was translated and published all over the world in a few days. In the early years of Khrushchev's time in power, the mid 1950s to 1964, he attempted economic reforms with mixed results. He ordered the cultivation of vast areas of virgin land requiring the mass movement of hundreds of thousands of workers from urban areas to the new farms. Besides unsettling large numbers of people at both ends, the agricultural production from the new areas was modest at best. Bureaucratic requirements remained and, as an example, if a peasant wanted to slaughter a cow, he had to get permission from no less than seven officials. On the industrial side, Khrushchev also attempted major changes by moving thousands of managers from central offices in Moscow to the plant sites all over the vast country. This might have been a good management initiative if it had been done with better planning and more gradually, but typical of Khrushchev's impetuousness, it was done all at once. The result was chaos and intensive infighting among the top managers. Industrial production did not increase, and in some areas it declined. To a growing number of political elite, Khrushchev appeared to be a man who flitted from one reform to another, and sometimes back again.

Of course Khrushchev was blamed for these failures, and the inner circle of Soviet leaders were not afraid to privately criticize him, as they never would have Stalin. However, he was given an opportunity in November 1956 to assert Soviet control through military power when a grassroots independence revolt developed in Budapest, Hungary. After several days delay, Soviet troops already in the country used heavy weapons including tanks to ruthlessly put down the rebellion. While criticized abroad, Khrushchev was solidly supported at home, especially by a unified military. NATO complained but did nothing. Offsetting the disgrace of the suppression of Hungary, in the world's eyes, were the successful launch in 1957 of the first satellite, *Sputnik,* to orbit the earth, and in 1960, the first manned satellite piloted by Yuri Gagarin.

Unfortunately for Khrushchev these triumphs were not enough to save his Premiership, especially after the disastrous confrontation with America over missiles in Cuba in 1962. Prior to that, he had been required to seek permission from the Presidium to build a wall between the Soviet and western sectors of Berlin to prevent the exodus of Berliners who were moving out to the west. These humiliations were too much for the Soviet power structure. So in October 1964, Khrushchev was summoned to appear before the Central Committee of the Party and was charged with various offenses. Leonid Brezhnev presided, and it was clear to all, including Khrushchev, that Brezhnev had the support to remove him. Unlike the Stalin days when a former high official would have been immediately killed, or at least sent to a *gulag,* Khrushchev was allowed to resign and go into quiet retirement.

Leonid Brezhnev was the premier of the Soviet Union from 1964 to his death in 1981. Brezhnev's eighteen years in power were noteworthy primarily for almost total lack of economic improvement, but a very aggressive foreign policy, especially toward the eastern bloc countries. In looking back, many Russians refer to this period as the "era of stagnation." Brezhnev was not a man of ideas, and certainly not of reform, but he lavished personal benefits on himself and a few close to him. A story, perhaps true, is illustrative: Brezhnev was showing his mother several large, expensive homes that he had acquired, when he asked her what she thought of them. She replied they were very nice—but what would he do if the communists came back in power?

Although Brezhnev was willing to accept a *détente,* a lessening of tension, with the US, he did not hesitate to enforce Moscow's will throughout the Soviet bloc. In 1968 communist reformers took over the Czechoslovak government. Because they were communists, Brezhnev vacillated for a few months but then came down hard on the rebels. He proclaimed the Brezhnev Doctrine, which basically said the Soviet Union had the right to intervene militarily in any Soviet state that was threatening the welfare of the whole union. Obviously, this made the Cold War even more frigid.

Brezhnev's end came in death, but his power and internal prestige declined precipitously after he launched a costly war in Afghanistan that most Soviet citizens did not understand or support. The army had to endure a humiliating retreat. Because of the war and decades of centralized economic policies, the economy of the Soviet Union was near collapse. During the next few years, until 1985, the country had minimal direction, but then a truly transformational leader was appointed—Mikhail Gorbachev.

Espionage During the Cold War.

International spying certainly did not begin during the cold war. Both British and Soviet spy networks were very active and quite sophisticated in the 1930s. This time especially provided a fertile environment for the recruitment of those in Britain, mainly intellectuals, who believed the capitalist economic system was not working and would soon be replaced. Of course, this was the time of the worst worldwide depression for the vast majority of people, but also a time when wealthy classes still controlled much of European society. It was not a stretch for some socially minded but privileged individuals at universities to see communism as the superior alternative.

It is important to distinguish initially between the two main types of espionage: human source intelligence (HUMINT) and signals or electronic intelligence (SIGINT). This overview will consider only HUMINT espionage, but it is fair to say that SIGINT successes had far greater impact in a military sense than all the human spy operatives. Just two examples will make this case. The cryptanalytic work that was done by the British at Bletchley Park north of London during World War II had an immeasurable impact on military operations by both the British and American forces throughout the war. The German military code, transmitted through the Enigma Machine, was broken at Bletchley and the secret of the breach was kept by those who knew. As a result, the Germans would continue to use the code unawares until the final days of the war.

Another example was the American code breakers who deciphered the Japanese naval code in 1942, enabling US naval forces to have knowledge ahead of time about Japanese naval operations. These SIGINT methods may to some be less interesting than human operations, and today they are among the most secret activities of technologically advanced countries. Still, HUMINT holds the most compelling and dramatic attraction for millions of readers of both fiction and non-fiction. As mentioned, the 1930s and 1940s were a time when Soviet recruitment of British citizens to spy for the Soviet Union against their own country was unusually successful. The so called "Cambridge Five" are a classic example of just this point. At Cambridge University in the mid 1930s many students and some faculty were strongly sympathetic to socialism and communism. Four individuals—Kim Philby, Donald Maclean, Guy Burgess, and John Cairncross—were recruited, directly or indirectly, by a faculty member, Anthony Blunt. They left the University and sought positions in the British government in diplomatic and intelligence fields. All were successful and moved up the line to increasingly sensitive positions. They were ideologically committed to the Soviet Union and, for many years, supplied the Soviets with secret intelligence covering different areas, including military and economic planning.

All were eventually uncovered. Maclean and Burgess escaped to Russia in 1953, followed much later by Philby in 1963. Blunt and Cairncross admitted their spying activities but were not prosecuted because they cooperated with British investigators. It was a huge embarrassment to the British intelligence community because of the great length of time it took to discover the "moles" in the system. One reason for this, offered by some observers, is that it was just very difficult for many well born, highly educated Englishmen to believe their colleagues were traitors.

On the other side, there were virtually no Soviet citizens who were recruited to spy for the British or Americans against their country. However, a few defectors volunteered their services and proved to be extremely useful, especially in identifying Soviet spies in the western country's intelligence services. Two of these defectors were Anatoliy Golitsyn, who identified Philby, and Oleg Gordievsky who fingered Cairncross.

It is safe to say that espionage will always be a part of international competition, but the methods and technology will constantly change. What we actually know about current espionage activities is that they are similar to icebergs: what we see and know is only a fraction of what actually exists.

CHAPTER 8

European Resistance to Communism

French and Italian Political Resistance

ALTHOUGH THE RESISTANCE to the military expansion of communism through the establishment of NATO and the American doctrine of containment, both previously discussed, were largely successful, there were other significant efforts to elect communist governments by entirely peaceful and democratic means. Two examples of this were the creation of communist political parties in France and Italy. The French Communist Party, known as the PCF (*Parti communiste francais*), was founded as early as 1920. The PCF had broad support among intellectuals, students, workers, and anti-capitalist liberals. However the Party had limited success in electing officials nationally because of an inability to unify with other likeminded political parties, such as the Socialist Party. There were also divisions within the European communist parties themselves between those, like the PCF, who saw themselves as independent and essentially French, and those communists who were part of the international movement controlled by the Soviet Union. During the 1930s the intellectual support for communism grew rapidly because of the worldwide economic depression. Many people saw communism as a vehicle to protect humane and liberal values. However, World War II changed that for most people. With the power and expansion of the Soviet Union and the establishment of NATO by the Western countries, most governments and political philosophers were forced to choose sides.

The PCF actually reached its zenith in membership with over half a million members in 1946 and received the most votes in the National Assembly elections that year. There were many observers, including Under-Secretary of State Dean Acheson of the US, who believed that the PCF would soon become the first democratically elected communist government in Europe. But such was not to be the case. The United

States imposed severe restrictions regarding access to Marshall Plan assets on governments outside of the Soviet sphere, if they were controlled by communist political parties. Because of these restrictions the PCF was forced to withdraw in May of 1947 from the majority French government. Consequently, it grew closer to Moscow and more vociferous against the ruling party in France, calling it the tool of American capitalism.

During the 1950s, the PCF was outside of the French government and largely isolated but remained faithful to the principles of communism. In 1958 the Party opposed the return of Charles de Gaulle to the presidency, but during the following decade they found ways, from time to time, to support him. The PCF was never again a significant force in French politics and, after the brutal response of the Soviets to the Hungarian and Czechoslovak independence demonstrations, the Party moved away from Moscow and identified more with Eurocommunism, an unofficial group of communists not directed by Moscow. After the fall of the Soviet Union in 1991, many European communist parties formally dissolved, but not the PCF. It remained in existence but was marginalized by other left wing groups such as the Socialist Party and the Greens.

The Italian Communist Party, the PCI (*Partito Communista Italiano*), was always much larger and more influential than its sister the PCF. While both parties were started in the early 1920s, the PCI attained a membership of over two million in 1947. One of the reasons for the success of the communists in Italy was the hash reaction toward the PCI by Mussolini and the Fascists, who outlawed the Party and persecuted its members. Many PCI members reacted by becoming very active in the resistance against Mussolini and the Nazis. As the war wound down, those fighting the Fascists became very popular among ordinary Italian citizens and communism was seen as far preferable to totalitarian dictatorships.

After the war the PCI was active in helping to write and adopt a democratic constitution and was a major participant in the government, although never part of the majority. These efforts created a political split with the Soviet Union, but the PCI remained connected financially to the Soviets. After the Hungarian revolt in 1956, PCI membership divided almost equally between those who believed the insurgents were counter-revolutionaries who needed to be put down, and those who saw Russia's response as oppressive. Still the Party membership remained impressively large; the US estimated in 1960 that the PCI membership was over 1.3 million, making it the largest communist party in western Europe. In 1969 the split with the Soviets became, as a practical matter, complete. The Secretary General of the PCI, Enrico Berlinguer, attended a conference of international communist parties in Moscow, and directly told Brezhnev that the suppression of Czechoslovakian reform was a tragedy. He also stated that his Party disagreed fundamentally with the Soviets on such questions as national sovereignty and socialist democracy. During the late 1970s and all of the 1980s, the PCI was definitely affiliated philosophically with Eurocommunism. Consequently, when the Soviet Union and its official connection to communism collapsed in 1991, the dissolution of the PCI was a foregone conclusion.

At mid-century, it seemed quite possible that the political success of the communist movement in Europe might be realized. No two countries exemplified this more than France and Italy. Both had suffered tragically in the war and both were slow to recover economically, creating fertile possibilities for radically different policies. However, the communist parties of both countries were ultimately unsuccessful. One major reason for this, although certainly not the only reason, was the brute efforts at control and the physical oppression used by the Soviets against the eastern European countries within their control.

Greek Civil War

Unlike the French and Italian communist movements, the communists in Greece were initially more inclined to seize power by revolutionary means. The civil war in Greece was essentially a two-phase war. After the Nazi occupation ended in October 1944, a communist-led resistance group established a provisional government which rejected the Greek king and his government-in-exile. The king was supported by the Democratic National Army group and, more importantly, by Britain. The royalist army immediately challenged the communists and fighting broke out. The British intervened and forced a settlement, but it was tenuous at best. Further fighting ensued, but by February 1945 the British had subdued the communists and a general election was held in March. The communists abstained from voting, and consequently a royalist majority was elected. The king was returned to Greece the following year. This ended the first phase of the civil war, but there was much more to come.

The second phase of the war began in March 1946 and lasted until August 1949. The communists, who were known as the EAM-ELAS (which stood for the National Liberation Front) launched a full scale guerrilla war against the government. Britain was again faced with the international obligation to defend the monarchist government from a take-over by EAM. Of course, by 1946 all of the World War II combatants, including Britain, were demobilizing, and their populations were not at all sympathetic to a new war, no matter where it was located. The British made efforts to encourage de-escalation, or a cease fire, but the communists recognized the weak military and financial situation of the British and refused to lay down their arms. The British called on the United States to honor the newly declared Truman Doctrine of containment of communism. On March 12, 1947, President Truman asked the US Congress for funding and authority to support the Greek government in their struggle with EAM. This was the first, but not the last, military activity by the US in resisting the spread of communism.

The US did not involve itself in the fighting in Greece but supplied massive amounts of military equipment and important financial backing to the Greek government. A big question in many western minds was what Stalin would do to support the Greek communists. On this point, timing was on the side of the anti-communists. In the late 1940s the Soviet Union was also recovering from a horrendous war and had all it could handle dealing with the occupied areas of eastern Europe that it controlled. Stalin was still willing to assist political efforts of communist movements, as in France and Italy, but not military wars outside of its sphere of interest.

The Greek Civil War dragged on from mid 1947 to mid 1949, when EAM was finally overwhelmed and most of its members left Greece. For a small country the human suffering was shocking. It is estimated that more than 50,000 people died and over 500,000 were displaced from their homes. This hard won victory over communist forces was solidified by the creation of NATO with Greece as a charter member.

After World War II, the struggle against communism in western and some parts of central Europe was less a contest of competing ideologies than it might have been in the 1930s. The world had seen in vivid contrast the evils of totalitarianism, first from the Nazis and shortly thereafter by the Soviet Union. Democracy and capitalism were viewed by most as the only reasonable alternatives to other forms of government, even if for some this was by default. A ravaged Western Europe had many serious economic and societal problems, but the overwhelming majority of ordinary people craved freedom and an opportunity to prosper.

CHAPTER 9

The Collapse of the Soviet Union and Modern Russia

The Impact of Mikhail Gorbachev

AFTER LEONID BREZHNEV died in 1981, the Soviet Union was virtually leaderless. Two premiers were selected, Iu. Andropov and K.U. Chernenko, who both served a very short time and died within thirteen months of each other. It was clear to most Politburo members that a much younger man needed to be selected. And the obvious choice was Mikhail Gorbachev, who was the next highest member of the Communist Party's Central Committee. Gorbachev, at age 54, was named General Secretary of the Party in 1985, a position tantamount to the leader of the government.

Gorbachev was indeed a major change from all previous Soviet leaders. He was intelligent, well educated, a lawyer, but had spent his entire career as a Communist Party functionary. Although thoroughly committed to Marxism-Leninism, he was respected as open minded and pragmatic. The new premier was the most worldly-wise of any previous Russian leaders and his ability to adjust to unfamiliar situations surprised many foreign leaders. Even his wife, Raisa, was well educated and westernized. The couple made a powerful first impression on many diplomats outside of the USSR.

Probably most important of all, Gorbachev had an understanding of global economics and of the USSR's rapid downward spiral. The ruble had been experiencing double digit inflation for several years and was essentially rejected in international markets. Due to decades of centralized economic planning and overemphasis on military hardware, many technologies to improve efficiency and productivity had been ignored. This was true across the board from industry to agriculture. Consequently, basic food and consumer products were in short supply, and a ubiquitous black market existed in spite of government efforts to control it.

On the political side, party corruption and general undermining of Soviet authority brought to a head the dramatic collapse of the Soviet Empire. This collapse was greatly accelerated by the accession to power of Gorbachev. In what proved to be the last great attempt to reform the Soviet system, Gorbachev immediately began the most remarkable changes that the Soviet Union had witnessed since the 1920s. Although it was never his intention to destroy either the communist party or the Soviet Union, these reforms loosed forces that, within seven years, would force Gorbachev to retire from office and would end both communist rule and the Soviet Union as it had existed since the Bolshevik revolution of 1917.

Dynamic leadership was needed to deal with the nation's economic decline and political disarray. Most understood that the country was in trouble and needed to be revitalized. The six years during which Gorbachev was in power were an extraordinarily confusing period. Could communism reform itself, in the process becoming democratic, without abandoning socialism? Or was the rot in the communist regime so deep-rooted that the entire system had to be abandoned before a more efficient and decent order could be created? In 1986 Gorbachev began his move toward the left by adopting a policy of *glasnost*, a vague term that literally means publicity or openness, but that soon acquired a variety of meanings. There was a new tolerance of the distribution of information and opinions on a wide range of issues in Soviet newspapers, journals, and television. Taboo subjects such as Stalinist terror, censorship, degradation of the environment, corruption, and crime began to appear regularly in publications available to all.

Nevertheless, the most pressing problem for Gorbachev was the economy, which continued to deteriorate after he assumed leadership. In the agricultural industry, long the Achilles' heel of the Soviet economy, he replaced many managers and officials, revised production procedures, but retained central control of the collective farms. Unfortunately, he did not encourage private enterprise of small plots to incentivize increased production. Sixty plus years of centralized planning and management was not to be changed over-night. Gorbachev and his economic advisors also realized early on that industrial production would continue to fall behind the West unless advanced technological equipment could be rapidly introduced. The scientific knowledge existed in the Soviet Union in the 1980s to improve commercial technology, but the engineers and financial resources were still being absorbed by the military-industrial sector. The hardliners and the military strongly resisted any serious reallocation of resources.

Gorbachev's inability to revive the economy undermined his other achievements, which were impressive. At no previous time in the history of the USSR did the people enjoy as much freedom as they did in the late 1980s. Although the Soviet Empire had begun to unravel, Gorbachev's skills and his commitment to peaceful reform remained intact. He was thoroughly dedicated to the preservation of the Soviet Union and socialism and made every effort in behalf of both causes. Also important in terms of world peace were the personal relationships that Gorbachev established with two world leaders: President Ronald Reagan of the US and Prime Minister Margaret Thatcher of Britain. He met with Reagan in Geneva in 1985 and again in Reykjavik in 1986. The purpose, particularly of the Reykjavik meeting, was nuclear disarmament and general reductions in military buildup. Both issues were critical to the Soviets because of their deteriorating economic problems and the fact that Reagan, who had recently been reelected, was increasing defense expenditures dramatically. There was also talk of a US Strategic Defense Initiative (SDI) that would develop an intercontinental missile defense system capable of destroying Soviet long range missiles in flight. If developed, this would have significantly changed whatever remained of the balance of power between the two superpowers. Although they reached no agreement in the 1986 meeting, the two world leaders did sign a nuclear treaty a year later in Washington that required both powers to destroy all ground-based nuclear weapons. All available evidence indicates that this treaty has been honored by both sides.

Gorbachev's policies regarding the Eastern bloc countries were often confused, some believed contradictory. For instance, he allowed significant levels of self-governance over local matters but was firm in opposing any ideological changes that might threaten the communist state. He had previously condemned the Soviet repressions of Hungary and Czechoslovakia but made no moves to encourage any independence or autonomy among the eastern bloc countries. Consequently, beginning in 1989 the countries of the Eastern Bloc—Poland, East Germany, Bulgaria, Rumania, Hungary, and Czechoslovakia—broke away, declared their independence and discarded communism without encountering any forceful attempt by the Russians to restrain them. The influences and changes that occurred in Poland are illustrative of the powerful feelings of rejection of Soviet occupation in other Eastern Bloc countries.

"Solidarity" was the name of the first Polish trade union that was authorized to exist in the eastern bloc without strict control from any communist party. This was done in August of 1980 in order to keep the shipyards operating in Gdansk (previously Danzig). A year later a union leader, Lech Walesa, was elected president of Solidarity. He quickly became an international figure because he expanded the union's demands well beyond labor issues, into peaceful protests for freedom and democracy. Solidarity was firmly supported by the Polish Catholic Church which tied the union's positions to Catholic social teachings. Pope John Paul II reinforced this connection when he visited his homeland of Poland in June of 1983. The Pope was greeted by more than one million Poles in a stadium in Warsaw where he specifically referred with favor to Solidarity. The ruling communist party of Poland was, from that time forward, under an international microscope and in no position to impose repression on the workers of Poland. A few years later, in November of 1989, "The Wall," which had prevented people from moving out of the Soviet sector, began to be dismantled. The Soviet Union as an empire was destroyed forever.

To sum up the six plus years of Mikhail Gorbachev's time as leader of the Soviet Union is not simple because this period in Russian history was as complex as the man himself. It can be argued, as some historians have, that Gorbachev's intentions were honorable and beneficial, such as his policy of *glasnost* and non repressive response to the Eastern Bloc countries. His failures are blamed on intense resistance from hardliners at home and the deep malaise created by seemingly impossible economic woes. However, there is another side that must be considered: he never abandoned his faith in Marxism as an economic principle and tried to the end to force reform through a failed concept. Moreover, Gorbachev tried to satisfy both the left and the right of the power structure, usually alienating both. It is certainly clear, though, that Gorbachev instituted changes that would never be reversed and that millions of people in Russia and eastern Europe are better off today because of them.

Boris Yeltsin, the Disappointing Hero

During the years prior to the ascendancy of Gorbachev to the premiership, he and Boris Yeltsin had been allies and opponents on more than one occasion. Gorbachev tolerated Yeltsin because he saw in him a charismatic leader, particularly in Moscow, who could help to promote the reforms that were necessary. However, Yeltsin angered many Politburo members with his self promotional style and aggressive anti-corruption efforts. When Gorbachev became General Secretary in 1985 he was persuaded to demote and isolate Yeltsin, but by 1989 Yeltsin had managed, with the help of Gorbachev, to return to an important position as President of the Republic of Russia. Even though Russia was by far the most important Republic, this was clearly a subordinate position to those who held power over the entire Soviet Union,

Yeltsin's golden opportunity came when right wing communist members of the Politburo launched a coup against Gorbachev in August of 1991. He was placed under house arrest at his *dacha* outside of Moscow, but the plotters made several mistakes, the most important of which was not to secure the support of the military. Gorbachev simply returned to Moscow. The coup leaders began to lose their nerve, many disappeared. The army was ordered to surround the Kremlin, which it did, but when ordered to fire on protesters against the coup, the military refused. Yeltsin, who was on the scene, took full advantage in front of live television coverage from all over the world by standing on a tank in Red Square and denouncing the traitors who led the coup.

The attempted take-over failed after three days, but that was not enough to save Gorbachev's government. He did not resign immediately, but Yeltsin, who was now an international hero, made the most of his position as President of the Republic of Russia by proclaiming Russia as independent of the Soviet Union. The vast majority of common Russian citizens applauded this action. The Soviet Union without Russia was, of course, unthinkable, and so the other Soviet republics (Ukraine, Georgia, Armenia, Belarus, Kazakstan and the other "Stans" in Asia, also broke with the mother country. Some were capable of self reliant independence but others were still dependent on Russia for fuel and other necessities. Relations between the former republics and Russia remain tense and uncertain to this day. How could a superpower empire that had effectively dominated much of Europe for over forty years have collapsed so quickly? Yeltsin offered an explanation: "The world can sigh in relief. The idol of communism, which spread everywhere social strife, animosity, and unparalleled brutality, which instilled fear in humanity, has collapsed."

The enormity and complexity of problems that faced the new, modern Russia after 1991 would have been enough to challenge the most skilled administrator, but clearly that description did not fit Boris Yeltsin. As with his predecessors, Yeltsin's most urgent and difficult problem was the economy. Gorbachev had tried to move from the centrally controlled and publicly owned means of production to what he referred to as, "democratic socialism." However, Yeltsin decided to take the huge step to a completely free market and rapid transfer of government enterprises to private ownership. His economic advisors anticipated that there would be some inflation and devaluation of the ruble, but they were dismayed to see what ensured: within two months of implementation, prices had soared ten times previous levels, the value of the ruble had declined dramatically on the international market, and unemployment had risen rapidly. The lot of the Russian people until 1995 was miserable. Alcoholism, always a problem, increased dramatically, and life expectancy decreased from 75 to 71 for women and from 65 to 58 for men.

The process of privatization of major industries went quickly but was fraught with corruption; ultimately a few very wealthy and powerful individuals controlled large parts of the economy. Obscenely displaying their newly acquired wealth, they were derisively referred to as "the oligarchs." Many also occupied senior positions in the Yeltsin government. Yeltsin, who was never popular with the Politburo, likewise had many enemies in the newly created Parliament. Inevitable struggles between the President and Parliament reached a climax in 1993 when Parliament leaders sought to impeach him. Convinced that he was still popular, Yeltsin arranged a referendum on his policies. Fifty-nine percent of the voters expressed confidence in Yeltsin as President. Failing in this peaceful approach, the Parliament leaders barricaded themselves in the Parliament building, issuing statements deposing Yeltsin and appointing two of their members as Acting President and Defense Minister. Yeltsin ordered dispersal from the building and then surrounded it with loyal army troops. After a few shots were fired, the leaders of the attempted coup surrendered and were eventually convicted and sentenced to prison terms. In a little over two years, Yeltsin had faced down two attempted coups. Unfortunately for Russia, this did nothing to ease economic difficulties.

In 1995 Yeltsin was elected to a second term as President, but the pressures of office and his barely concealed alcoholism were taking their toll on his health. After his five years in office, few had illusions about him. He was seen accurately as impulsive, authoritarian, and isolated. He had no new ideas left but was too stubborn to change any previous policies. However good news was coming: by the second half of the 1990s the economy was improving. Privatization had produced many more consumer goods and available food products than had ever been produced under communism. Corruption was still rampant and too few were benefiting significantly from an improved economy, but many citizens could see a light at the end of the long tunnel.

Yeltsin had serious heart surgery at the end of 1996 and, although he recovered, his energy level, always one of his strengths, was never the same. His political influence declined with his health and lessened activity. By 1998, Russia had defaulted on its international debt obligations and most Russians were envious of their neighbors to the west. Yeltsin acknowledged the obvious and resigned effective on the last day of the century, December 31, 1999. However, even his final act had a profound long term effect on Russia: he appointed Vladimir Putin to the presidency.

The history of Russia and the Soviet Union is a fascinating study, but no period offers greater extremes and fundamental changes than the 20th century. In little over seventy years Russia's government literally went from a radical left-wing, authoritarian, dictatorship to a partially democratic, capitalistic, and largely open society. Major problems remain, and the trend led by Putin appears to be reversing some of the steps forward. Clearly, however, for Russia there will be no returning to anything close to its Byzantine past.

Genocide in Bosnia

Bosnia-Herzegovina is one of the countries that separated from Yugoslavia after the death of Tito in 1980. It is located on the eastern side of the Adriatic and is bordered to the southeast by Serbia. It contains three ethnic groups in roughly equal numbers: Serbs (Orthodox Christians), Croats (Catholics), and Albanians (Muslims). These groups had never lived together in harmony, and during the 1980s there were many episodes of violence and sectarian abuse.

In Serbia, a powerful former communist, Slobodan Milosevic, gained control of the former Yugoslav army and began a campaign of nationalism and religious hatred toward all who were not Serbs and Orthodox Christians. In 1992, Milosevic turned his attention to Bosnia, where the Serb population amounted to approximately 32% and had protested that they were victims of Muslim discrimination and atrocities. There never was compelling evidence to support these claims but that did not stop Milosevic. His army invaded and captured Sarajevo, the Bosnian capital. Sarajevo soon became a killing ground with Serb snipers shooting helpless civilians in the street, eventually killing over 3500 children and an unknown number of adults. The Serbs were particularly cruel to Muslims, using rape against women and girls and murdering men and young boys by the thousands These atrocities were referred to as "ethnic cleansing."

The United Nations and the US complained, imposed useless economic sanctions, and offered peace conferences, all to no avail. However, on February 6, 1994 the world's attention focused on Bosnia when a mortar shell exploded in a market in Sarajevo killing 68 and wounding nearly 200 innocent people. The US, under President Bill Clinton, organized NATO to issue an ultimatum to the Serbs to withdraw their artillery from Sarajevo and comply with a NATO imposed cease-fire. Milosevic and the Serbs responded by taking hundreds of UN peacekeepers hostage and turning them into human shields. Atrocities and genocide continued until finally, in August of 1995, effective military intervention began with a massive US led NATO bombing campaign to drive the Serbs out of Bosnia and to destroy their military infrastructure in Serbia. Muslim-Croat troops occupied Bosnia and Milosevic agreed in November to peace talks in the United States. This ended the first major NATO military operation in the organization's nearly fifty years.

CHAPTER 10

Rise of the European Community

The Need for Unity

ONCE RECONSTRUCTION OF the war-torn countries of western Europe had begun, the leadership of some of the largest economies agreed that there was an urgent need for economic unification. This movement started in the early 1950s between France, Germany, and Italy through an association dealing with the production and distribution of coal and steel. The problems that were impeding growth were the cross border restrictions of transportation, tariffs, labor movement, and political concerns. But to many European citizens it was not at all clear why they should get closer together. They spoke different languages, had different traditions and ways of life. It seemed that what separated them was far more important than what they had in common.

Still, other European nations, including many smaller countries in the north, were added but they, from the beginning, were concerned that the larger nations would overwhelm their interests and control the organization to their own benefit. However, the smaller countries, such as Ireland, Austria, the Netherlands, and Portugal, did benefit quite well economically from what was then called the Common Market. These benefits took the form of access to low interest debt for economic development. Another always present issue in the Common Market was the reluctance of most nations to hand over national sovereignty to a central, and virtually anonymous institution over which ordinary people had no control. It was clear some countries had greater influence than others in Brussels, the capital of the Common Market.

Some post war egos and jealousies continued to thwart true unity. In 1963 and again in 1967, Charles de Gaulle, President of France, personally vetoed British efforts to join the union. His stated reason seemed specious to most, that Britain was too closely tied to the US to support the Common Market wholeheartedly. But Britain and many other countries did join in the 1970s so that prior to the collapse of the Soviet Union there were fifteen European members. After the opening of eastern Europe, ten more joined and today there are twenty seven members with several applications pending, including Turkey.

In 1992 an important Treaty was signed by the Common Market members in Maastricht, Netherlands which: created a central bank, established a completely free trade zone, changed the name to the European Union, and set the stage for the introduction in 1999 of a common currency, the euro. There was great optimism in Europe in the years before the 21st century about a "European Model" that would set the Continent apart from the United States and would be a powerful economic engine moving into the new century. When the 27 countries of the EU are considered as a single trading entity, they do generate the largest Gross Domestic Product (GDP) in the world. Unofficial numbers for 2011 reflect that the EU had a GDP of 17.5 trillion in US dollars with a modest 1.6% growth rate for the year. That compares to the US economy that created a GDP of slightly more than 15 trillion dollars and growth of 2.8%.

But great optimism led to a step too far. The so called European "elite," those financiers, industrialists, and political power brokers who exercised considerable influence over the EU decided that a strong central government with sovereign powers and supported by a constitution was needed. Such a constitution was presented to the membership in 2004 and, to the shock of the elite, it was defeated by large margins in France and the Netherlands. Other countries, including Britain, withheld votes on the constitution which has never been adopted. So the EU is structurally the same today as it was at the turn of the century, but huge financial problems for the eurozone countries currently exist and this is a central focus of Chapter 11.

Immigration

It became very clear by the mid 1980s that the face and character of Europe was changing demographically. There had always been guest workers and immigrants, but most of them had been European in origin: Italians, Spaniards, Portuguese, and Yugoslavs. But now many new immigrants came from the Middle East, Africa, and Asia. Although some sought political asylum, they had no intention of returning to their homelands.

In the decades before 1980, the movement of people followed three main patterns: the migration from the countryside into the cities; the displacement of virtually entire Jewish populations from eastern Europe and Germany; and decolonization. Although the migration to the cities has slowed somewhat, the percentage of city dwellers in western Europe is approximately 75%. The loss of Jewish populations has deprived Europe of some of it's most vibrant intellectual, religious and cultural life. A third major migration was decolonization, which can be described as the return of Europeans from colonial countries upon those countries achieving independence. While perhaps not true immigration, the impact on countries such as France, which received more than one million returning people from Algeria in 1962, created an overwhelming economic challenge. Similar decolonization was experienced by Britain and the Netherlands.

The impact of these demographic changes, while temporarily negative, did not typically raise the more difficult and long term problems of lack of assimilation and cultural identity. These problems are at the heart of the massive movement of Middle Eastern, East African, and Asian Muslims into western Europe beginning in the 1980s. Many Muslims had no desire to integrate into European societies the way earlier immigrant waves had done. This resistance to assimilation created increasing social, political, and cultural problems. Thus, overnight what had been considered a relatively minor and local problem was becoming a major political issue with growing resistance on the part of native populations. Perhaps they were wrong to react in this way, but they had not been aware until recently of this trend and no one had ever consulted them. The problems facing west European societies were more often than not the second and third generation immigrants who revolted against their adopted country. The reasons given are poverty, overcrowding, unemployment, and lack of education.

As an example, France is now home to the largest Muslim community in Europe, approximately 5.5 million. This number has doubled since 1980. French policy towards its Muslims has been based on principles of secularism and assimilation. There is the French belief in a homogeneous society with tolerant multiculturalism. Secularism and culture are an impediment to Muslim assimilation because religion has always been an integral part of Muslim identity. Clear evidence of this is the fact that in the mid 1980s there were 260 mosques in France, and today there are over 2,000. So the French model has not worked as well as expected. There were riots in 1994-95 in the French Muslim communities of Northern France and Paris. Although there were indications that the situation in the immigrant community was under control, closer observers noted that the situation was continuing to smolder. By the year 2000, half of the inmates of French prisons were of Muslim origin. There were further riots in November of 2005 and, although religious issues were a factor, most experts estimated that the economy was the major motivating factor.

The German approach to its immigration problem involved well-intentioned people and institutions who promoted integration. These groups included social workers, academic researchers, churches, and political parties. The primary ethnic group immigrating into Germany were Turks who settled mostly in the major German cities such as Berlin, Cologne and Duisburg. They came primarily from the least developed parts of Turkey and were illiterate and far more conservative in their religious beliefs than Turks from Istanbul or Ankara. Thus it came as no surprise that, almost from the moment of their arrival in Germany, Turks confined themselves to their own kind and customs. The Muslim population of Germany today is approximately 3.6 million, of which Turkish immigrants comprise more than half.

While the aim of German policy has been the integration of the Turkish communities, the aim of Islamist organizations, supported by the Turkish government, has been diametrically opposed to integration. The Turks in Germany remain Turks even if they have adopted the German nationality and vote in German elections. There has been some rioting and property destruction in the German Muslim community, but the German economy has been markedly better than other European countries and that is a major reason for less upheaval.

The 1.6 million Muslims in Britain, mainly from Pakistan and Bangladesh, constitute about half of the post-war immigrant population in Britain. According to a variety of polls, a majority of British Muslims admitted that they were better treated in the United Kingdom than in other European countries. There was, for instance, no total legal ban in Britain, in contrast to France and Germany, to wearing the *hijab* in school or in public. London became the refuge of many extremists who had been sentenced to long prison terms, or even death, in their native countries in the Arab world. Britain also allowed radical organizations, which were banned in many Arab countries such as the Muslim Brotherhood, to operate freely. The attitude of British authorities was traditionally one of benign neglect. As long as the radical Muslim organizations did not commit flagrant breaches of peace, they were left alone. This began to change after the September 11, 2001 terrorist attacks in the United States and the July 7, 2005 underground bombings in London. British authorities took a more active interest in radical preachers who were inciting to murder. Some were deported and others sentenced to prison terms. Today Britain and the US share intelligence information about potential terrorist activities, and it is accurate to say that many planned attacks have been thwarted in both countries. The situation in all western European countries remains volatile with intense homeland law enforcement agencies watching immigrant societies closely.

The Welfare States

The drive for economic security is, psychologists tell us, one of the most important human desires. After World War II, this desire could not have been stronger among the masses of unemployed and impoverished of war—torn Europe. The first European nation to respond to this need was Britain through its Labour Party in the late 1940s and early 50s. Britain created universal health coverage through the National Health Service. The enactment of the law was more an acknowledgement of existing conditions because taxpayer funded health care was a fact of life for all but a few wealthy individuals who could afford private insurance. But it expressed a powerful change in British political opinion.

Other countries such as France, Italy, and Germany resurrected political parties that had been popular prior to the war. These parties were often called Christian Democratic parties because most members were active Christians and part of the working class. While there were wide differences of opinion among the members of the Christian Democratic parties on many issues, one subject received unanimous support, lifetime job security and pension guarantees.

One budgetary policy change, made by all western European countries that made it possible to fund increases in social welfare services, was an almost total elimination of defense spending. This was possible because of the creation of NATO and the reliance on the defense capabilities and expenditures of the United States. Generally, substantial economic growth across the west allowed many countries, including Britain, to expand social programs without great strain on their budgets. But by 1980, growth had slowed and even reversed for a time in most regions.

For the British, this resulted in a new government of the Conservative Party with a new Prime Minister, Margaret Thatcher. She was determined to roll back many socialist policies that had been enacted in the last two decades, and to reduce the power of trade unions throughout most industries. Her time in office (1979 to 1990) was marked by constant political battles over budgetary issues, but she and the Conservatives were successful in reversing the trend toward more generous government programs.

Thatcher's leadership was gradually followed across the Continent even by left-of-center political parties, like the various Christian Democratic parties of Germany and France.

Many ordinary Europeans resisted reductions in welfare benefits by comparing Europe to the US. This thinking dealt with the concept of the value of leisure time and economic security. The argument was that Europeans valued leisure more than Americans and that as a result, even though poorer, they had a better quality of life. However, many were persuaded that if they remained half as well off as Americans, this would mean poorer health care, education and a diminishment across all kinds of goods and services, and therefore a lower quality of life. There was certainly no broad consensus of opinion. There were those who strongly believed that reforms and cuts in welfare/social benefits had to be made. More and more, frequent questions were asked as to which of the services of the welfare state could be afforded at a time of slow or no growth and a rapidly aging population.

In addition to these problems, there was the long term trend in Europe of an alarming decline in the birthrate. In an article entitled *The End of Europe,* economist Robert Samuelson drew attention to the discrepancy in birth rates between Europe and America and pointed out that by 2050 one-third of the population of Europe would be 65 or older. Apart from high unemployment and slow growth, how could European economies operate in the future with so many elderly people heavily dependent on government benefits?

As contemporary economists see it, the modern European welfare state redistributed income from the working young to the retired old and from the rich to the poor. As an example, the British welfare state guarantees a minimum standard income and provides social protection in the event of job loss and services at the best level possible. This is the theory. In practice, services are at a low level and have to be rationed according to the funding available. The character of the welfare state varies from country to country. However, all European countries experienced the fact that the welfare state became more and more expensive primarily because people were living longer, medical costs became much more expensive, and rising unemployment meant fewer jobs producing revenue. Added to that, the number of students had grown five-fold all over Europe since the end of the Second World War. This necessitated more funding for schools and universities and a delay in youth employment to support the welfare state system. Taxes were raised across Europe; in France the overall tax rate reached 45%.

Economic stagnation at the end of the 20th century caused European higher education and scientific research, once foremost in the world, to be steadily declining. All this meant a further reduction in Europe's position in the world and, at the same time, less defense spending weakened its ability to be a military partner of the United States or even to project military power for peacekeeping purposes.

CHAPTER 11

Europe's Necessary Changes

THIS FINAL CHAPTER differs from the previous ten in that it is not history but rather a consideration of the current economic circumstances in the European Union, especially the eurozone countries. Obviously, this is a dynamic situation and what may be true today could change dramatically tomorrow. Indeed, as this is being written, there has just been a significant rejection by the voters of austerity measures in at least two eurozone countries, France and Greece. Nevertheless, the problems remain and their solutions are still elusive and controversial.

Pillars of Economic Growth

Noted international economist and political writer Fareed Zakaria has written in a *Washington Post* article titled, *Crisis of the old order,* about what he calls the three pillars of the old order. Zakaria describes them as characteristics of the old European order for any democratic, capitalist country to create and foster economic growth. The first pillar is the welfare state which would have the government protect the unemployed, aged, disabled, and poor. The second is an optimistic faith in constant growth which would raise everyone's living standards, and ultimately redistribute income more equitably. The third pillar is a reliance on global trade and finance that would serve all country's mutual interests. Unfortunately, Zakaria believes, "All three pillars are now wobbling."

This state of economic malaise has affected all of Europe, but because of the common currency, the euro, it seems to have more significantly hurt the 17 countries that use the euro. Those countries, with their current unemployment rates listed, include: Spain 24.1%, Greece 21.7%, Portugal 15.3%, Ireland 14.5%, Slovakia 13.9%, Estonia 11.7%, France 10.0%, Cyprus 10.0%, Italy 9.8%, Slovenia 8.5%, Finland 7.5%, Belgium 7.3%, Malta 6.8%, Germany 5.6%, Luxembourg 5.2%, Netherlands 5.0%, and Austria 4.0%. (Source: *Washington Post,* May 3, 2012.) While many of these countries are small and their economies are dependent on a few major sources, such as tourism, the list also includes some of Europe's major economic engines.

The unemployment rate for all eurozone countries is 10.9%, compared to the United States at 8.1%. So with the exception of a few major economies, Belgium, Germany, Netherlands, and Austria, it is accurate to say that the eurozone currently has serious unemployment challenges. Increases in unemployment can certainly be seen as a symptom rather than a cause of recessions, but it is critically important and must always be at the forefront of any discussion of recovery.

The first Zakaria pillar is the dramatic increase in welfare programs. All government spending, as a percentage of each country's GDP, provides a frightening picture of the increases in a relatively short time. In 1999 government spending accounted for 52% of GDP in France, 48% in Germany, and 30% in the US. By 2007, those numbers had increased to 52.6% in France, 43.9% in Germany (a small decrease), and 36.6% in the US. When one considers the fact that government spending in the US includes defense spending at much higher percentages than any European country, the increases for social spending are even more alarming for Europe. The solution to this part of the problem is fairly obvious: austerity measures in guaranteed income levels; gradual increases in age of retirement eligibility; greater shared health care costs; and overall reductions in the growth of government programs. These answers are well known on both sides of the Atlantic but elected officials in Europe and the US have shown little political courage to make necessary changes in policy. So the negative side of the equation is clearly established, but will austerity measures not prolong or increase the severity of an economic decline? Many experts think so.

Austerity vs. Government Stimulus

Although the economic declines in Europe and the United States were both similar and related, the governmental actions taken to respond to the crisis were virtually opposite. The US acted quickly and massively to stimulate the economy with monetary support to the financial sector and to state governments for infrastructure projects, helping to maintain the construction industry. Europe, in contrast, quickly turned toward austerity programs, cutting government spending in an effort to reduce budget deficits. Since these policies were implemented in 2009, the results are evident for all to see. The US economy, as measured by GDP, has grown slowly but steadily, with many experts believing this year will show a growth rate of between 2 and 3 percent. On the other hand, the eurozone is expected to contract by 0.3 percent this year. In most EU countries spending cuts have led to slower growth, lower tax revenue, and bigger deficits.

If one accepts the proposition that more governmental spending, not less, during down economies is the better approach, then the next question might be, what activities and programs return the greatest economic bang for the government's buck (or euro). Studies since the boom days of the 1990s have shown that spending on education has a big multiplier effect, and spending on R&D has created whole new innovative industries that have carried the US economy for more than a decade. But government spending in these areas has actually declined significantly.

Are there voices in America, and especially in Europe, that are advocating greater stimulus policies in the near term to prime stagnant economies? The British newspaper, *the guardian,* addressed this question on February 14, 2012 in an article titled, *UK austerity v US stimulus: divide deepens as eurozone cuts continue.* In the article, Labour Party leaders and business managers, not often on the same side, point out that in Britain the state must be willing to invest in infrastructure and public services, otherwise private investment will go abroad and conditions will worsen. There is a growing awareness that fiscal rigor and austerity policies are not working and that something has to give before a sovereign debt crisis impacts the UK. If these alarm bells are sounding for Britain, how much more critical is the impending crisis for France, Spain, and Italy? Likewise, the International Monetary Fund (IMF) and officials at Standard & Poor's rating agency have issued statements warning of the perils of quick and severe cuts.

The solution may be apparent to many but the political means to achieve that solution remains very difficult. A senior European diplomat says it is almost impossible to forge a consensus when the situations across eurozone economies are so varied. "The problem with this crisis is the Germans don't feel it . . . It's something happening somewhere else." Besides the political impediments, there is also the EU structural deficiency. There is no central control similar to the US Federal Reserve that operates outside of the political apparatus. The Federal Reserve is protected and allowed to make unpopular but necessary decisions. The EU has no lender of last resort.

There is the European Central Bank but its decision making is ultimately controlled by its three most powerful members; Germany, Britain, and France. The fear of a growing number of European economists is that it may already be too late to change course and that conditions will worsen before they improve. But what is the future of the euro?

Survival of the Euro—No Reasonable Option

Only a few years ago, the concept of the survival of the euro was not open to question. The euro was assumed by most to be either the strongest or second strongest single currency in the world. But a worldwide recession from 2009 to the present has changed that belief. Attitudes of many financial experts has moved from panic, to serious concern, and now to thoughtful efforts to find a solution to save the currency. In spite of continuing squabbling by politicians across Europe, some forward thinking writers are leading an effort to preserve the euro (*The Economist,* September 17, 2011). A four step short term and long term process has been proposed. First, any rescue must make clear which of the eurozone countries are solvent, which are solvent but illiquid, and which are bankrupt. Second, all of Europe's banks, both private and public, must withstand true stress tests to determine their ability to survive sovereign debt default. Third, efforts must be made to shift the eurozone's policies from its obsession with budget cutting and to move to an agenda of growth. Fourth, the EU, in the longer term, must design a new system of central control over irresponsible borrowing.

The first two steps are largely technical and are being done, but they both raise the issue of credibility. Through most of the last decade, both political and economic leaders ignored and even pretended that the problems of welfare costs, falling revenues, and commercial competition from Asia, were at most a cyclical anomaly. In the capitalist world of private investing, credibility is everything. Private investors cannot be forced to invest in anything including bonds issued by sovereign countries. So overly optimistic financials and other questionable marketing rarely influences professional investors. Honesty in evaluating the financial status of eurozone countries is critical. Those countries and their lending institutions which are solvent should assist countries and institutions determined to be illiquid. Illiquidity simply means that, while the entity's assets exceed its liabilities, it cannot pay its current liabilities on time or completely as required.

These entities can and must be returned to solvency. Bankrupt countries, and at this point it appears that Greece is the only eurozone country that meets this description, must either leave the eurozone or accept the harsh medicine of default and virtual elimination of borrowing for an unknown time to come.

The third step listed above has been considered in this chapter so it only needs to be said that there appears to be substantial support, outside of Germany, for a lessening of austerity measures and an increase in government support for growth programs. The fourth step is one that will admittedly take more time but is no less important. This required structural change is not just a eurozone problem but must involve all 27 EU members in creating a central and non-political control over sovereign borrowing. Efforts along these lines have been tried and been unsuccessful in the past, but recent experience has shown those rejections were mistaken. The very future of the European Union as a single trading entity, with a single currency, and strong central authority is at stake.

What would be the most likely impact of the loss of the euro, from whatever cause? All 17 eurozone countries would revert to their previous currencies but the values of those currencies would vary dramatically. The bankrupt or illiquid countries would certainly see an immediate devaluation of their currency. Greece would see, according to some authorities, a devaluation to approximately 1,000 drachma to the dollar. Others, such as France, Italy and Spain, would also see significant devaluations. These devaluations would actually help with their exports because their products would be cheaper, but individual and commercial investments would be essentially wiped out. Also borrowing would, in the short term, cease until the country recovered economically.

But a few eurozone countries like Germany and the Netherlands would probably experience an increase in value of their new currencies because of the overall strength of their economies. However, their exports would be hurt because their products would be more expensive, and the current tough competition with Asia to sell abroad would be made even tougher. Analysts have predicted that, with a euro break-up, the smaller and weaker countries could be faced with a 40-50% loss of GDP, and the stronger countries could lose 20-25% of GDP. *The Economist* estimates that a break-up in the single currency could cost trillions of euros, but the money needed to recapitalize European banks and some countries would be in the range of billions of euros. Stated that way, it seems a bargain.

It is almost unnecessary to say, but the greatest single impact from the loss of the euro would be the long lasting uncertainty in world fiscal centers and the resulting retrenchment in any financial activity with more than the most limited risk. This is not a formula for growth, but the opposite.

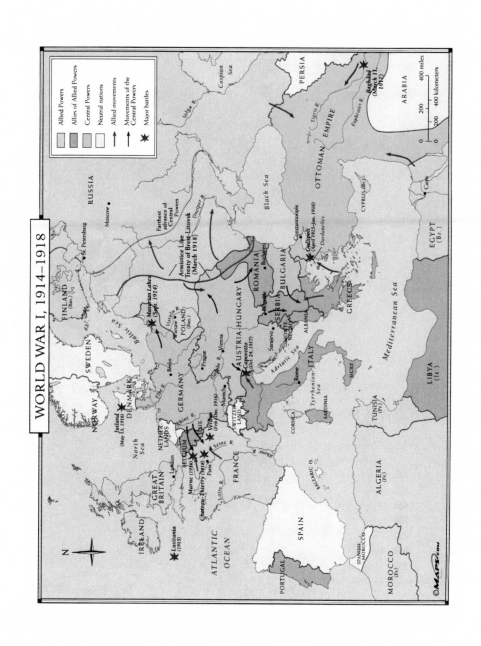

WORLD WAR I, 1914–1918

Legend

Allied Powers
Allies of Allied Powers
Central Powers
Neutral nations
→ Allied movements
→ Movements of the Central Powers
★ Major battles

RUSSIA

St. Petersburg

Moscow

Volga R.

Caspian Sea

FINLAND (Rus.)

Baltic Sea

Farthest advance of Central Powers

Dnieper R.

Armistice Line Treaty of Brest-Litovsk (March 1918)

SWEDEN

NORWAY

Masurian Lakes (Sept. 1914)

Vistula R.

Warsaw

POLAND (Rus.)

Black Sea

Constantinople

OTTOMAN EMPIRE

PERSIA

Tigris R.

Euphrates R.

Baghdad (March 11, 1917)

ARABIA

Dardanelles

Gallipoli (April 1915–Jan. 1916)

GREECE

ROMANIA

Bucharest

BULGARIA

Belgrade

SERBIA

MONTE-NEGRO

ALBANIA

Sarajevo

AUSTRIA-HUNGARY

Vienna

Caporetto (Oct. 24, 1917)

Danube R.

Prague

Elbe R.

Berlin

GERMANY

Munich

DENMARK

NETHER-LANDS

Jutland (May 31, 1916)

North Sea

IRELAND

GREAT BRITAIN

London

ATLANTIC OCEAN

Lusitania (1915)

BELGIUM

Soissons

Verdun (Feb.–Dec. 1916)

Rhine R.

SWITZER-LAND

Marne (1914)

Château-Thierry (1918)

Paris

Seine R.

FRANCE

Loire R.

Rhône R.

ITALY

Rome

Adriatic Sea

Tyrrhenian Sea

SARDINIA

CORSICA

SICILY

Mediterranean Sea

LIBYA (It.)

TUNISIA (Fr.)

ALGERIA (Fr.)

SPAIN

PORTUGAL

BALEARIC IS.

SPANISH MOROCCO

MOROCCO (Fr.)

EGYPT (Br.)

CYPRUS (Br.)

Cairo

N

©Maps.com

0   200   400 miles
0   200   400 kilometers

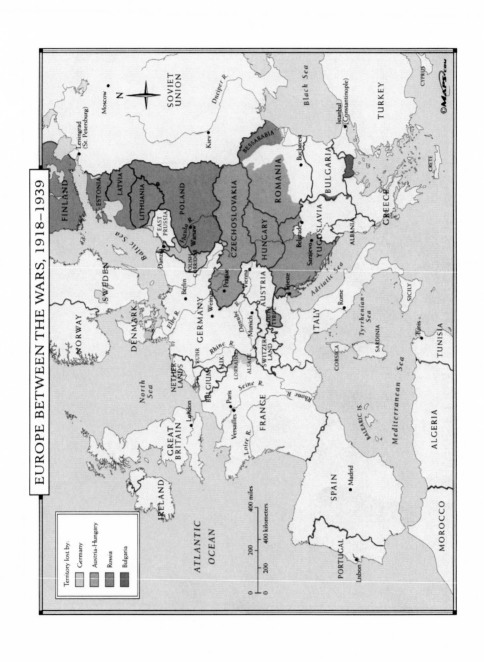

EUROPE BETWEEN THE WARS, 1918–1939

Territory lost by:
Germany
Austria-Hungary
Russia
Bulgaria

ATLANTIC OCEAN

IRELAND

GREAT BRITAIN

London

North Sea

NETHER-LANDS

BELGIUM

LUX.

Paris

Versailles

Seine R.

Loire R.

FRANCE

Rhône R.

SPAIN

Madrid

PORTUGAL

Lisbon

MOROCCO

ALGERIA

Mediterranean Sea

BALEARIC IS.

CORSICA

SARDINIA

Tyrrhenian Sea

Rome

ITALY

SICILY

Tunis

TUNISIA

NORWAY

SWEDEN

DENMARK

Baltic Sea

GERMANY

RUHR

Elbe R.

Berlin

Weimar

Munich

Rhine R.

Danube R.

ALSACE

LORRAINE

SWITZER-LAND

SOUTH TYROL

AUSTRIA

Vienna

Trieste

Adriatic Sea

FINLAND

Leningrad (St. Petersburg)

ESTONIA

LATVIA

LITHUANIA

EAST PRUSSIA

Danzig

POLISH CORRIDOR

Vistula R.

Warsaw

POLAND

Prague

CZECHOSLOVAKIA

HUNGARY

Belgrade

Sarajevo

YUGOSLAVIA

ALBANIA

GREECE

CRETE

Moscow

SOVIET UNION

Dnieper R.

Dniester R.

Kiev

BESSARABIA

ROMANIA

Bucharest

BULGARIA

Istanbul (Constantinople)

Black Sea

TURKEY

CYPRUS

N

0   200   400 miles
0   200   400 kilometers

©MAPS.com

COLD WAR EUROPE, 1946–1990

N

NATO Alliance

Warsaw Pact Nations

ICELAND

FINLAND

NORWAY
SWEDEN
Helsinki
Leningrad

Oslo
Stockholm

Riga

North
Sea

DENMARK
Copenhagen

Vilnius

Minsk

SOVIET UNION

IRELAND
Dublin

UNITED
KINGDOM

NETHERLANDS
Amsterdam

Elbe River

Rhine

London

Brussels
Bonn

BELGIUM

LUX.

Paris

Seine

Loire River

Berlin

EAST
GERMANY

WEST
GERMANY

Vistula R.

Warsaw

POLAND

Kiev

ATLANTIC
OCEAN

CZECHOSLOVAKIA

Prague

Munich

Danube River

Vienna
Bratislava
Budapest

Kishinev

FRANCE

SWITZ.
Geneva

AUSTRIA

HUNGARY

ROMANIA

Po River

Belgrade

Bucharest

YUGOSLAVIA
Sarajevo

BULGARIA
Sofia

SPAIN
(Joined NATO in 1982)

Tiber R.

Rome

ITALY

Skopje

Istanbul

Lisbon
Madrid

ALBANIA
(Withdrew from
Warsaw Pact in 1968)

Tirana

TURKEY

PORTUGAL

GREECE

Mediterranean Sea

Athens

ALGERIA

0   200   400 miles

0   200   400 kilometers

©MAPS.com

Bibliography

Chapter 1.

Anderson, Benedict, *Imagined Communities.* New York: Verso Books, 1991.

Cooper, Frederick and Stoler, All L (eds), *Tensions of Empire: Colonial Cultures in a Bourgeois World.* University of California, 1997.

Haugh, Richard, *The Great War at Sea 1914—1918.* Oxford University Press, 1989.

Ozment, Steven, Kagan, Donald, and Turner Frank M., *The Western Heritage,* 9th Edition, Pearson Prentice Hall, 2007.

Tuchman, Barbara, *The Guns of August,* Ballentine Books, 1962.

Chapter 2.

Ascher, Abraham, *Russia, a Short History.* New Edition, One World, 2009.

Baltzly, Alexander and Salomone, A. William, *Readings in 20th Century European History.* Appleton Century Crofts, 1950.

Fussell, Paul, *The Great War and Modern Memory.* Oxford University Press, 1989.

Garraty, John A. and Gay, Peter, *Columbia History of the World.* Harper & Row, 1981.

Haugh, Richard, *The Great War at Sea 1914-1918.* Oxford University Press, 1989.

Ozment, Steven, Kagan, Donald, and Turner Frank M., *The Western Heritage.* 9th Edition, Pearson Prentice Hall, 2007.

MacMillan, Margaret, *Paris 1919.* Random House, 2002.

Chapter 3.

Hanioglu, *Ataturk, An Intellectual Biography.* Princeton University Press, 2011.

Liggon, Helen, *The Civil War.* Wolfhound Press, 2006.

Moody, T.W. and Martin, F.X., *The Course of Irish History.* Roberts Reinhart, Revised, 2001.

Zurcher, Erik J., *Turkey: a Modern History.* I.B. Tauris & Co., 2005.

Chapter 4.

Acton, Edward, *Rethinking Russian Revolution.* Arnold, 1990.

Ascher, Abraham, *Russia: A Short History.* New Edition, One World, 2009.

Baltzly, Alexander and Salomone, A. William, *Readings in 20th Century European History.* Appleton Century Crofts, 1950.

Cornwell, John, *Hitler's Pope, the Secret Life of Pius XII.* Penquin Books, 2008.

Service, Robert, *A History of Twentieth Century Russia.* Harvard University Press, 1998.

Chapter 5.

Bosworth, R.J.B., *Mussolini.* Arnold Publishing, 2002.

Garraty, John A. and Gay, Peter, *Columbia History of the World.* Harper & Row, 1981.

Minehan, Philip, *Civil War and World War in Europe.* Palgrave Macmillan, 2011.

Overy, Richard, *1939: Countdown to War.* Penquin Books, 2011.

Ozment, Steven, Kagan, Donald, and Turner Frank M., *The Western Heritage.* 9th Edition, Pearson Prentice Hall, 2007.

Payne, Stanley G. *A History of Fascism, 1914-1945.* Univ. of Wisconsin Press, 1995.

Toland, John, *Adolf Hitler.* Anchor Books, 1992.

Chapter 6.

Garraty, John A. and Gay, Peter, *Columbia History of the World.* Harper & Row, 1981.

Hastings, Max, *Inferno, the World at War 1939-1945.* Alfred Knopf, 2011.

Ozment, Steven, Kagan, Donald, and Turner Frank M., *The Western Heritage.* 9th Edition, Pearson Prentice Hall, 2007.

Kennedy, David, *The Library of Congress, World War II Companion.* Simon & Schuster, 2007.

Olson, Lynne, *Citizens of London.* Random House, 2010.

Toye, Richard, *Churchill's Empire.* Henry Holt & Co., 2011.

Chapter 7.

Ascher, Abraham, *Russia: A Short History.* New Edition, One World, 2009.

Hitz, Frederick, *The Great Game, the Myths and Reality of Espionage.* Vintage Books, 2005.

Ozment, Steven, Kagan, Donald, and Turner Frank M., *The Western Heritage.* 9th Edition, Pearson Prentice Hall, 2007.

Panayi, P. and Lareres, K. Eds., *The Federal Republic of Germany since 1949: Politics, Society and Economy before and after Unification.* London, Longman, 1996.

Service, Robert, *A History of Twentieth Century Russia.* Harvard University Press, 1998.

Chapter 8.

Drake, Richard, *The Soviet Dimension of Italian Communism.* Journal of Cold War Studies, 2004.

Gilberg, Troad, *Coalition Strategies of Marxist Parties.* Duke University Press, 1989.

Kertzer, David, *Parties and Symbols, The Italian Communist Party and the Fall of Communism.* Yale University Press, 1998.

Minehan, Philip, *Civil War and World War in Europe.* Palgrave Macmillan, 2011.

Ozment, Steven, Kagan, Donald, and Turner Frank M., *The Western Heritage.* 9th Edition, Pearson Prentice Hall, 2007.

Thomas, Martin, *The French Empire between the Wars,* Manchester University Press, 2005.

Chapter 9.

Ascher, Abraham, *Russia: A Short History.* New Edition, One World, 2009.

Garton Ash, Timothy, *The Polish Revolution, Solidarity.* Yale University Press, 2002.

Ozment, Steven, Kagan, Donald, and Turner Frank M., *The Western Heritage.* 9th Edition, Pearson Prentice Hall, 2007.

Service, Robert, *A History of Twentieth Century Russia,* Harvard University Press, 1998.

Chapter 10.

Kuisel, Richard, *Seducing the French: The Dilemma of Americanization.* University of California Press, 1997.

Laqueur, Walter, *The Last Days of Europe, Epitaph for an Old Continent.* St. Martin's Press, 2007.

Samuelson, Robert, *The End of Europe.* Washington Post, June 15, 2005.

Chapter 11.

The Economist, *How to save the euro.* September 17, 2011.

The guardian, *UK austerity v US stimulus: divide deepens as eurozone cuts continue.* February 14, 2012.

Zakaria, Fareed, *Crisis of the old order,* Washington Post, November, 2011.

Index

H

Hemingway, Ernest 47
Hindenburg, Paul von 43-44
Hitler, Adolf 25, 38-39, 42-47,
    50-55
Holocaust 55

J

Jellicoe, John 21
Joffre, Joseph 19
John Paul II, Pope 71
Jutland 21-22

K

Kamal, Mustafa 21, 27, 30, 34
Khrushchev, Nikita 60-61
Kilmainham Gaol 31

L

Lateran Treaty 41
Lausanne Peace Treaty 30
League of Nations 25
Lenin, Vladimir 34-37
Lloyd George, David 24-25, 29, 32
Ludendorff, Erich 23

M

Maclean, Donald 63
Marshall, George 53, 57, 65
Milosevic, Slobodan 74-75
Minehan, Philip 48
Moltke, Helmut von 18
Mussolini, Benito 40-43, 47, 54, 65

N

NATO 30, 57, 59-60
Nicholas II, Czar 15

O

Orlando, Vittorio 24
Ottoman Empire 27, 30

P

Papen, Franz von 43
Pearse, Padraic 31
Pershing, John 23
Philby, Kim 63
Pius XI, Pope 41
Putin, Vladimir 74

R

Reagan, Ronald 70
Reichstag 43-44
Rhodes, Cecil 13
Roehm, Ernst 44
Rommel, Erwin 54
Roosevelt, Franklin 53, 55

S

Samuelson, Robert 81
Scheer, Reinhard 22
Schlieffen, Alfred von 15
Schlieffen Plan 15, 18, 20, 52
Solidarity 70-71
Sputnik 61
Stalin, Joseph 36-39, 46-47, 50-56,
    58-61, 67
Strategic Defense Initiative (SDI) 70

The author will make available a complimentary PDF of questions and issues that arise from each chapter. This can be used for discussion purposes by those who have a deeper interest in the causes and results of significant decisions taken during this turbulent century that literally transformed Europe. If you wish to receive this PDF, contact the author at artdrea@comcast.net.

Edwards Brothers Malloy
Thorofare, NJ USA
July 11, 2013